scarves

to make

scarves

to make

LINDA LEE

The Taunton Press

cover photo: Jack Deutsch

Taunton
BOOKS & VIDEOS
for fellow enthusiasts

Text ©1998 by Linda Lee
Photographs ©1998 by Jack Deutsch
Illustrations ©1998 by The Taunton Press, Inc.

Printed in the United States of America
10 9 8 7 6 5 4 3 2 1

The Taunton Press, Inc., 63 South Main Street,
PO Box 5506, Newtown, CT 06470-5506
e-mail: tp@taunton.com

Distributed by Publishers Group West

Library of Congress Cataloging-in-Publication Data

Lee, Linda.
Scarves to make / Linda Lee.
p.   cm.
SBN 1-56158-256-5
1. Scarves.
TT667.5.L44 1998
646.4'8—dc21   98-3972
CIP

acknowledgments

*As owner of The Sewing Workshop in San Francisco
I have the privilege of meeting and collaborating with some of
the best sewing professionals in the country. I want to thank
all the teachers at The Sewing Workshop and especially the
artists represented in this book (many of whom teach for me)
for their enthusiasm for this project and their unique
contributions to the art of sewing.*

*Thanks also to Jolynn Gower, acquisitions editor at
The Taunton Press, for her idea to do this book and for her
unending support and confidence. And, finally, thanks to
Darchelle Woltkamp and Stephanie Valley, without
whose daily assistance in my office I would be far less
productive and generally helpless.*

contents

beads and baubles 74

stenciled, stamped, and stitched 92

architectural shapes 120

introduction

Some of the most fascinating work in textile design and creative thinking shows up in the scarves produced by contemporary sewing artists. Whether they make scarves to sell or to wear themselves, I haven't met an artist yet who doesn't like a great scarf.

The scarf is such an all-purpose accessory. Whether for warmth or for show, no other accessory expresses a personality quite like a scarf. Making a scarf is the perfect project for practicing and perfecting a craft. A scarf is relatively small, requiring only a modest financial investment, and can usually be created in a short amount of time.

I selected the 13 artists whose work is presented here for their uniqueness in the sewing and art world. Each artist brings to the book a look that is signature to their style, a new approach to traditional techniques and materials, and a loosening of conventional sewing standards. From scarves of fabulous fabric with simple, but fine finishing details to scarves made from ordinary fabrics transformed by dyeing, stamping, or stitching, these artists have reinterpreted our vision of a scarf.

basics

basic sewing kit

Precision work requires good tools and the right equipment. The following essentials are recommended to have on hand for scarf making and for other fine sewing or craft projects. Buy the best you can afford and add to your store of equipment often. Find a space to work that has excellent light and adequate room to cut out and that, preferably, will allow you to leave your project out when you're not working on it.

tools for measuring and marking

Rulers, tapes, and other measuring devices provide the accuracy needed for exact cutting and consistent sewing. There are lots of marking tools on the market today. Test a few brands from each group and have several on hand for various fabric types.

tape measure You'll need a narrow, flexible fabric tape from 60 in. to 120 in. long to measure large areas. It's useful to have the numbers marked on both sides with the numeral 1 at opposite ends.

rulers Made of wood, plastic, or metal, large rulers are useful for measuring pieces of fabric, and smaller ones aid in drawing or cutting along a solid edge for straight or bias cutting. A clear plastic 2-in. by 18-in. ruler with a painted measurement grid is a popular size for multiple uses.

45° right-angle triangle Used primarily for marking and cutting bias, these clear or colorful translucent plastic utensils are available in many sizes.

seam gauge This 6-in. metal ruler has an adjustable marker that slides along the ruler and stays in place to record a measurement. It is handy for marking small measurements such as seam and hem allowances during construction.

chalk markers Available in pencil, block, or powdered-dispenser form, these tools highlight pertinent markings temporarily. Use white and light colors such as yellow or pale blue; stay away from red, which won't always come out of the fabric. Use for free-form markings or next to a straightedge ruler on the right side of fabrics.

erasable pens Marking pens in this category are either air-erasable or water-soluble and last for varying lengths of time depending on the fabric and the type of marker. Mark on the right or wrong side of the fabric, but test the pen's disappearing characteristics on a scrap first.

tracing paper and tracing wheel Tracing paper is a waxy paper used in conjunction with a tracing wheel to transfer necessary markings to multiple layers of fabric. Purchase a good-quality paper whose markings won't fade away when ironed but will disappear when laundered or dry-cleaned. Test the paper first! Tracing wheels are available with smooth or serrated wheels. Generally, this type of marking equipment will mar sheer and delicate fabrics and should be avoided.

"Hera" marker This plastic or bone marker leaves an impression in the fabric with no residue or color remaining. It is perfect for silk, sheer, and other delicate fabrics.

tools for cutting

As home sewing has become more professional, so have the tools for cutting. Where we once owned one pair of scissors for all purposes, there are now several choices as well as alternatives to scissors, depending on the fabric, the project, and the ease of use.

scissors and shears Bent-handled shears in 8-in. or longer lengths cut fabric with the least number of strokes and with nice straight edges. Straight-handled scissors in 7-in. or shorter lengths are good for trimming,

clipping, and grading. Duck-billed appliqué scissors are designed to trim close to stitching without cutting the wrong surface; they are also useful for grading. Microserrated scissors have a fine serrated edge on each blade that "grabs" the fabric and prevents fabric creep. It is not unreasonable to expect to use three or four different kinds of scissors or shears in the construction of one project. Keep the blades sharp (have them sharpened by a professional).

rotary cutter and cutting mat Sharp blades mounted in plastic housings make short work of cutting through multiple layers of fabrics, whether thick or thin. Rotary cutters are available in many shapes and sizes, some ergonomically designed, and the blades cut smoothly. Blades with novelty cutting designs are also available. A cutting mat is required when using a rotary cutter. Purchase a good-quality, self-healing mat with a 1-in. grid pattern and 45° lines marked on it.

seam ripper This fine-point ripper with a razor-sharp cutter delicately removes stitches without tearing the fabric. Some seam rippers even have a light at the end of the tool to illuminate fabrics sewn with dark thread. The finer and sharper the cutter, the better.

weights To experiment with a layout or to cut out without pinning, use weights to hold tissue or fabric pattern pieces in place. Plastic-coated discs, painted whimsical metal objects, and fabric-covered pellet tubes are just some of the varieties available.

tools for sewing

The most important piece of equipment in your sewing space is, of course, a sewing machine that is a workhorse and performs perfectly. A serger is a wonderful accessory to have, but it's not necessary in constructing the projects in this book. Having the right collection of presser feet (see the sidebar below) and other sewing aids simplifies your tasks and adds to the pleasure of it all.

pins New, good-quality pins are important for clean, unblemished pinning. Throw away your tired pins and buy new glass-head silk pins. The glass heads are easy to pick up and will not melt near heat; their fine points will not damage better fabrics.

needles Needles are much like pins—they need to be fine and extra sharp. For hand sewing, look for good-quality Japanese or English needles with eyes that are easy enough to thread. For machine sewing, keep a good

---

special presser feet

The standard presser feet that come with your sewing machine are the primary feet that you'll need to make the projects in this book. But newly designed specialty feet aid in the sewing process, improve your technical skills, and, in some cases, speed the process.

buttonhole foot
A buttonhole foot has two indented channels on the underside of the foot to allow each side of the satin-stitched buttonhole to slide through while sewing, preventing the stitches from "hanging up."

darning foot
This foot is a small full circle or an open-edged circle that allows you to see the direction of the stitching pattern easily and stitch small, delicate

designs without turning the fabric. The feed dogs are dropped, and the technique used is freehand embroidery.

edgestitch foot
This foot is a regular presser foot with a metal blade through the center. When fabric is placed next to the blade and the needle position is moved, the blade guides the fabric and allows you to stitch a straight line very close to an edge with little trouble.

embroidery foot
An embroidery foot has an open toe to aid in seeing decorative stitches as they are sewn and to follow premarked motifs easily.

supply of standard needles in all sizes from 60/8 to 90/14. Other specialty needles to have on hand include topstitching needles (110/18), jeans sharps for extra-fine fabrics, microtex needles for unusual fabrics and the new synthetics, needles for metallic threads, and leather needles for real and faux suedes and leathers. Change the needle whenever you change fabric type and after every project.

beeswax Passing a strand of thread through a cake of beeswax and melding the wax into the thread with heat (using an iron) prevents tangling and knotting and adds strength when hand sewing.

sewing machine You don't need a fancy machine with lots of extra stitches and features to make the scarves in this book. It is important to have a reliable machine with a good-quality stitch that sews on a variety of fabric thicknesses and weights and sews with many kinds of thread, including decorative.

serger Though you can make almost all the scarves in this book without one, a serger is a wonderful machine that's certainly nice to have. A serger should overlock a very flat, medium-wide three- or four-thread stitch formation with perfection on all types of fabrics from chiffon to wool. A differential (the ability to alter the upper and lower fabric feeding) is essential.

tools for pressing

To produce professional scarves, it's essential to develop good pressing skills. Use the right equipment for the task and the fabric and press frequently throughout the construction process.

iron Just as a sewing machine needs to be reliable, so too does an iron. Look for a properly weighted iron with a cleanable sole plate, multiple levels of dry or moist heat, and lots of steam when you want it. This is one time when the more expensive the iron the better the quality.

press cloths Using a press cloth helps to prevent fabric shine, scorching, and iron marks. The fabric dictates the type of press cloth—sheer cotton/poly for delicate and fine fabrics, heavier duck-type cloth for heavy fabrics. Always test your iron on the fabric before beginning the construction.

hemming feet
Fabric is automatically rolled into the edges of hemming feet to create perfect rolled hems. There are several widths to choose from. Placing the fabric in the right position and keeping it there takes practice.

patchwork foot
When you want a perfect ¼-in. seam or hem, the narrow width of this foot helps you to execute it with precision. Notches engraved on the toe of the foot indicate when to turn a corner exactly ¼ in. from the end.

pintuck foot
This foot has several grooved channels on the underside. Three-groove, five-groove, and seven-groove configurations are available. Double needles are used in conjunction with pintuck feet. After sewing one row of double-needle stitching, the tucked row that is formed is fed through one channel of the foot so that subsequent rows are parallel.

walking foot
Sometimes called an even-feed foot, a walking foot allows the top layer of fabric to feed through the sewing machine at the same speed as the bottom layer and prevents fabric creep. This foot is especially useful when sewing velvet and other pile fabrics and for matching plaids.

templates Lightweight cardboard such as tagboard can be cut into shapes for use as pressing templates. For hems, cut a 2-in. by 18-in. piece and draw horizontal lines in ¼-in. increments. Place the template on the wrong side of the fabric. Bring the raw edge of the fabric up and over the straight edge of the template, aligning it with a marked line the same width as the finished hem, and press through all layers. Templates can be any shape (curves, points, straight edges) to ensure precision pressing, especially in slippery fabrics.

clapper When placed over a steamed section of fabric, this hardwood block helps to remove the moisture from the fabric quickly. A clapper also aids in pressing a seam or edge more crisply.

point presser Small, trimmed seam allowances are best pressed open first over a narrow strip of wood with a pointed end before turning the seam to the inside. Point pressers are sometimes mounted on a clapper for a two-in-one piece of equipment.

sleeve board A sleeve board is a two-level padded surface shaped like a small ironing board that's useful for pressing seams and other details in a tube. It prevents unwanted press marks where the fabric folds and where the iron is wider than the fabric strip.

a glossary of stitches

You need to have a repertoire of stitches, both machine and hand, to handle fabrics effectively. Take the time to learn how and when to use them. It's worth it!

basting

Basting is a temporary stitch either by hand or machine used to prepare seams and other details and hold the fabric in place until permanent stitching can be done. Remove the basting thread before pressing or use silk thread, which does not leave a mark when pressed. Always baste just inside the permanent stitching line. Hand basting stitches include the following:

even basting Even basting is generally used for long seams and in areas that are stressed and need to be controlled. Space stitches evenly, ¼ in. long and ¼ in. apart, beginning and ending with a backstitch rather than a knot.

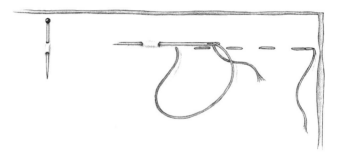

uneven basting Uneven basting is used for marking and for holding fabric together that's not stressed, such as a hem. Take a long stitch on the top surface and a shorter stitch through the fabric.

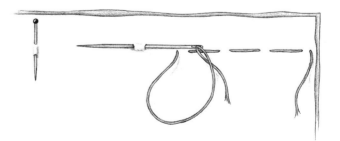

diagonal basting

Diagonal basting is used to hold fabrics together that are difficult to work with and tend to creep, such as velvet, corduroy, and slippery silks and satins. Take short stitches through the fabric at a right angle to the edge, spacing them evenly. You'll see diagonal stitches on the top and short horizontal stitches on the underside.

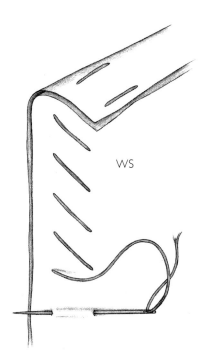

WS

chainstitch

A chainstitch, or thread chain, is a series of looped and interlaced stitches linked to form a thick, secure thread. Securely fasten a double thread to the fabric with one or two overlapping stitches. Form a loop on the right side by taking another short stitch. Slip the thumb and first two fingers of your left hand through the loop while holding the needle and thread end in your right hand (a). Using the second finger of your left hand, pick up a new loop and pull it through the first loop (b), tightening the loop as you proceed (c). Continue to work the chain to the desired length. Secure the free end with several small stitches (d).

edgestitch

A line of stitching an even distance from a folded or seamed edge. It holds an edge in place and/or adds a decorative element.

finish

This term refers to a variety of methods used to neaten an edge when it's not enclosed. Common finishes are serged (overlocked), zigzagged, pinked, turned and stitched, and bound with bias tape, fabric, or Seams Great bias mesh tape.

half backstitch

This stitch is used to understitch seams to prevent edges from rolling toward the outside. Bring the needle through the fabric to the upper side. Take a stitch back about ⅛ in., bringing the needle out again ¼ in. from the beginning of the first stitch. Take another stitch ⅛ in. and continue in the same manner.

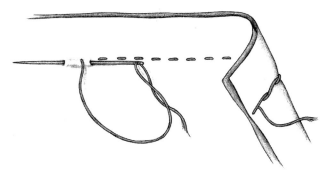

a

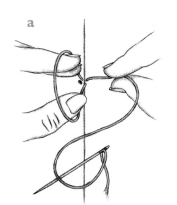

b

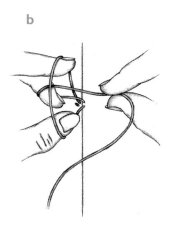

c

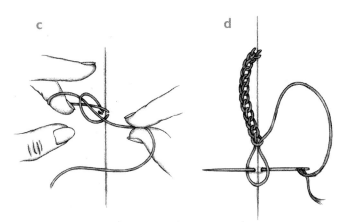

d

prickstitch

This variation of a backstitch is a hand stitch commonly used to insert a zipper, but it produces a decorative stitch as well. Carry back the needle only one or two threads (or any desired distance), forming a tiny surface stitch with a reinforced understitch.

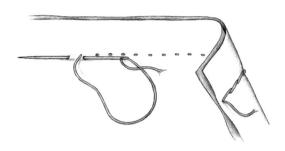

slipstitch

This invisible hand stitch is used to hem, hold trims in place, and close openings. Slide the needle through the folded edge and at the same point pick up a thread of the under fabric. Continue in this manner, taking stitches ⅛ in. to ¼ in. apart and spacing the stitches evenly.

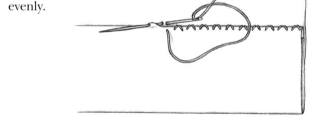

tailor's tacks

This method of marking through a single or double layer of fabric is used when other methods of marking would mar the fabric and when working with soft-surfaced fabrics such as velvet. Using a double strand of thread without a knot, take a single small running stitch through the fabric. Then sew another stitch across the first, pulling the thread until a large loop is formed. Gently roll the top layer of fabric back and cut the threads between the layers, leaving tufts on either side.

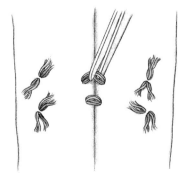

topstitching

Topstitching is sewn on the right side of the fabric and is meant to be decorative, whether subtle or dominant. Thicker threads in interesting fibers such as rayon can be used in tandem with special needle sizes.

understitch

When a seamline is pressed to form an edge that encloses the seam allowances, the underside should be understitched. Press the trimmed seam allowances to one side. From the right side, half-backstitch or machine-stitch close to the seamline and through all the seam allowances.

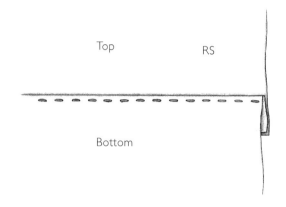

whipstitch

This is a bandstitch used to hold two finished edges together. The needle is inserted at a right angle from the back to the front, encasing the edge.

fabric preparation

Each fabric selected for your scarf should be studied carefully. Know the fiber content, learn about the care of the fabric, and understand the use of the final piece so that you can prepare your fabric accordingly.

preshrinking

It's always a good idea to preshrink fabric before you cut it out. In the case of scarves, pretreat the fabric in the same manner that you will clean the finished scarf. Laundering, dry-cleaning, and steaming are the methods used to prepare fabrics. Most fabrics can be laundered either by hand or by machine, even those that are traditionally dry-cleaned such as silk, wool, and velvet. Experiment with a scrap of fabric first. Simply heavily steaming a piece of fabric will emulate dry-cleaning without the expense.

straight of grain

Often the success or failure of a sewing project is directly related to whether the fabric has the correct grain, which means that the crosswise and lengthwise threads are at perfect right angles to each other. In order to check the grainline, the true crossgrain needs to be established. This can be done by tearing the fabric if it is a natural fiber or by pulling and removing a crosswise thread and cutting along the resulting space. Fold the fabric lengthwise, matching selvages and the fabric ends. If the edges do not align on all three sides, the fabric is off-grain and must be straightened.

Fabric can be straightened by steam-pressing the threads into proper alignment. With the fabric folded lengthwise, right sides together, pin every 5 in. to a padded surface such as a blocking board or ironing board along the selvages and ends. Press firmly, stroking from the selvages toward the fold.

Another method is to pull the fabric gently but firmly in the opposite direction from the way the ends slant until a perfect right-angle corner is formed. Sometimes a combination of the two methods can be used.

---

special handling of sheer fabrics

Sheer fabrics such as chiffon and georgette and other opaque silk fabrics require special techniques and materials when cutting out to ensure that they will hang on the straight of grain. Because they are so slippery, these fabrics need to be held in place and not be allowed to move all over your cutting table.

Cover the cutting surface with white paper that's gritty on one side and smooth on the other (such as examining-room paper). Lay a single layer of fabric on top of the paper, aligning the selvage with the long edge of the paper and the torn or cut edges with the ends of the paper. Staple or pin every few inches all of the edges of the fabric to the paper. Use a chalk marker to determine the cutting lines. Use microserrated scissors to cut through both the fabric and paper. These specialized scissors grab the fabric and inhibit the fabric creeping away from you as you cut. Mark each piece with tailor's tacks or with a Hera marker before removing the fabric from the table.

---

construction techniques

Building a repertoire of sewing construction techniques increases your awareness of the options and helps you choose the appropriate method for your fabric and style.

hems and edges

Hems and edges define the look of a scarf, from casual to formal, and finish the edges for long-term wear. Although raw edges have their place in today's design, it is generally considered preferable to enclose raw edges and finish by hand or machine.

handkerchief hem

Use this hem, also known as a narrow hem, on cotton and linen and other crisp fabrics. Turn ¼ in. to the wrong side and press. Turn up the edge again and press. Stitch by machine through all thicknesses.

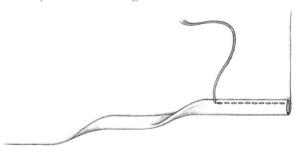

baby hem

Use this hem on delicate and fine fabrics such as silk, chiffon, and georgette. Staystitch ⅜ in. from the raw edge. Turn ⅜ in. to the wrong side along the staystitching line and edgestitch next to the folded edge. Using small trimming scissors or appliqué scissors, trim the excess fabric close to the stitching. Turn the edge up again and edgestitch. The finished hem is approximately ⅛ in. wide.

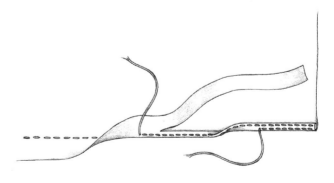

rolled hems

by hand—Machine-stitch ¼ in. from the raw edge and trim close to the stitching. Roll approximately ⅛ in. of the edge between thumb and forefinger, concealing the stitching. Stabilize the roll with the third and fourth finger and slipstitch, taking a single thread at each stitch. This is considered a couture edge.

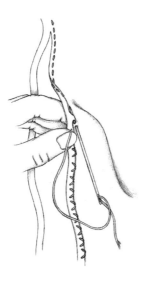

by machine—Most sewing machines have special presser feet that allow a fabric edge to feed through a cone-shaped section, rolling the fabric and stitching it down at the same time.

by serging—Many sergers have the added feature of rolling an edge and overcasting it with either two or three threads.

seams

Standard seam allowances used for the projects in this book are ½ in. wide unless otherwise noted.

trimming

Seam allowances should be trimmed only where less bulk is desired. For an enclosed seam, seam allowances should be trimmed to ¼ in. When two seams intersect at a right angle or at other corners, trim diagonally.

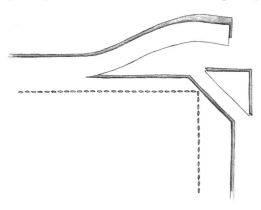

grading

When seam allowances are enclosed and turned together, trim each layer a different width to reduce bulk.

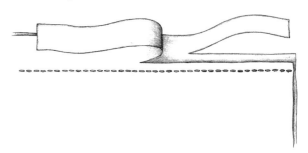

clipping

Curved seams require special trimming and clipping in order to lie flat. Trim an outward curve to ⅛ in. On an inside curve, clip into the seam allowance at even intervals. The tighter the curve, the closer the clips.

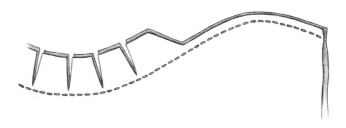

intersecting seams

Special sewing and trimming techniques are necessary when two seams cross. Stitch one seam and press open. Stitch the second seam in the same manner. Pin the two seams with right sides together, using a pin point to match the crossed seams exactly at the seamline. Then pin on either side of the seams and stitch. Trim corners diagonally.

guides for sewing straight seams

Mark the seamline with a line of chalk and stitch over the marking. Hold the fabric taut behind the presser foot with one hand and guide the fabric in front of the presser foot with the other hand.

Attach a magnetic seam guide to the throat of your sewing machine and align the edge of the fabric with the guide edge.

flat-fell seam

A self-finished seam, this version of the flat-fell seam can be completed without the use of a sewing-machine felling foot. Press one-half of the seam allowance to the right side (a). Trim one-half of the seam allowance away from the other side of the seam (b). With right sides together, position the trimmed edge inside the pressed edge. Stitch through all layers, close to the raw edge (c). Open the fabric with wrong sides up and press the seam to one side, covering the raw edge. Stitch the seam close to the pressed edge through all layers (d).

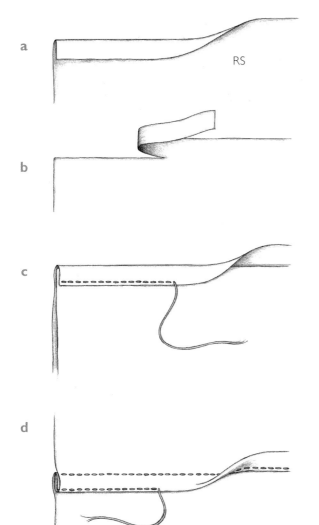

mock flat-fell seam

This method creates the look of a traditional flat-fell seam but is easier to sew. Sew a standard seam with the rights sides together. Trim one side of the seam allowance to about ¼ in. Press the seam to one side, covering the trimmed edge. Topstitch ¼ in. from the seam through all layers.

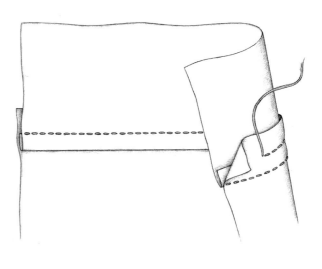

French seam

This enclosed seam looks like a plain seam on the right side and a small tuck on the wrong side. With wrong sides together, stitch ⅜ in. from the seamline in the seam allowance. Trim to ⅛ in. With right sides together, stitch along the seamline (¼ in. from the creased seam), encasing the raw edges.

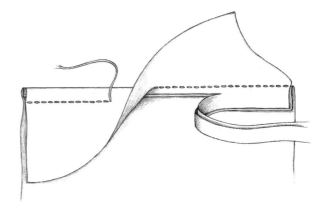

corners

Carefully crafted corners mark the difference between professional and homemade. Use sound techniques to sew precision corners.

reinforcing a corner seam

When stitching a straight piece of fabric to a corner, first staystitch through the portion of the seam that will need to turn the corner. Clip to the point. With right sides together, pin both sections with the clipped section up and stitch, pivoting at the point.

piped seams

Seams and edges become more defined and interesting when decorative piping is inserted.

right-angled corner

Baste piping to the right side of the fabric along the seamline, matching raw edges. Clip through the flange to the cording at the corner. Stitch, pivoting at the clipped corner.

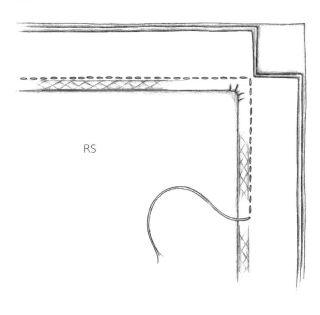

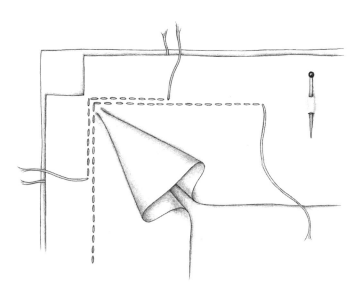

right-angled corner

When joining two corresponding pieces of fabric, shorten the stitch length for about 1 in. on either side of the corner.

acute-angled corner

If the corner is at an acute angle, take one or two small stitches across the point, depending on the weight of the fabric.

curve

Stitch the piping to the right side of the fabric, matching the raw edges. Clip through the flange to the cording at regular intervals to allow the piping to fit the curve smoothly.

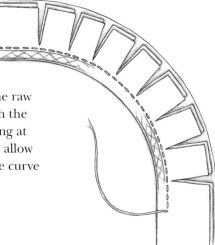

miters

Sewing a miter on an outside corner is the cleanest way to finish an edge. There is also less bulk than an ordinary folded corner.

square corners

Turn all seam or hem allowances to the inside and press (a). At the corner, open the seam or hem allowances and turn to the inside diagonally across the point and press (b). With right sides together, stitch through the diagonal line. Trim to ¼ in. (c). Press the seam open over a point presser (d). Turn to the outside, press, and topstitch (e).

sewing specialty fabrics

The luxurious fabrics of today and the innovative weaves and blends of fibers require special skills and tools to produce professional results.

velvet

Sewing two pieces of velvet together is difficult, but sewing one layer of velvet to a smooth fabric is even more challenging. Slippage and creeping are common problems. Some tricks that will reduce frustration include knowing that you need to baste, baste, baste. Diagonal basting using silk thread is the best method. Use a walking foot, roller foot, or Teflon foot and sew in the direction of the nap. You may need to decrease the pressure on the presser foot and hold the fabric taut while stitching. Match the weight of the thread to the weight of the fabric. You may need to use embroidery-weight cotton thread or 100% silk thread.

silks and sheers

Slippery fabrics such as chiffon, crepe de chine, georgette, charmeuse, and even some fine rayons require special handing. Some basting may be required, but more important, use good-quality sharp needles in small sizes such as 60/8, 65/10, or 70/12. Buy good-quality thread (100% cotton embroidery or 100% silk), reduce your stitch length, and hold the fabric taut while sewing. You can use a product called Perfect Sew to stabilize the stitching lines, as long as you are willing to launder the fabric to remove it after sewing.

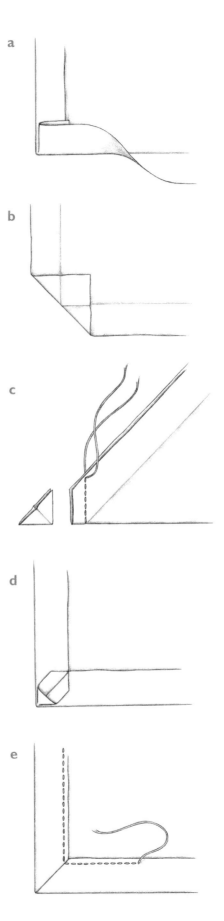

a

b

c

d

e

single-faced band

With right sides together, stitch a ½-in. seam starting and stopping stitching ½ in. from each end (a). Press the band away from the center. Stitch the adjacent band to the edge, starting at the seam of the previous band and ending ½ in. from the other end (b). Fold diagonally through the corner matching raw edges. Draw a diagonal line on the band, extending the line formed by the fold of the center (c). Stitch on the marked line, starting at the previous stitching and taking care not to catch the seam allowances (d). Trim the ends of the band ½ in. from the stitching. Press the miter seam allowances open (e). Press the remaining seam allowances toward the band.

a

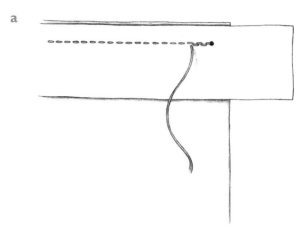

b

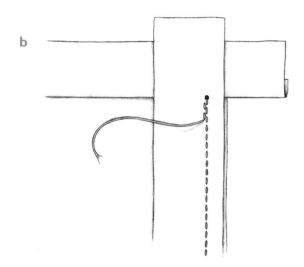

c

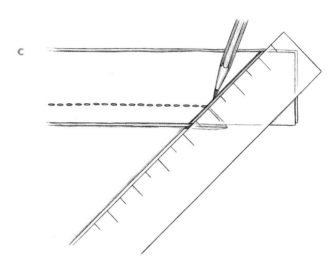

d

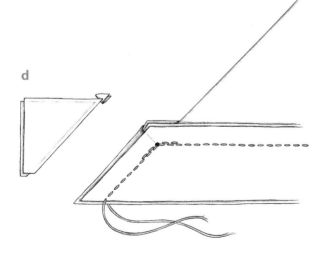

e

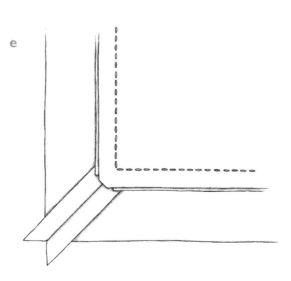

double-faced band

Begin by cutting a strip of fabric four times the finished width of the band. Press the strip in half lengthwise. Then press each raw edge to the center crease line (a). With right sides together, align the raw edges and stitch along the first crease line (b). End the stitching at a point that equals the finished width of the band. Back-stitch. At the ending point of the stitch, diagonally fold the band away from the edge at a right angle and then fold the band straight down, matching the fold to the two raw edges and aligning the other raw edges (c).

Keeping the opposite raw edge folded to the center crease, draw an arrow from the previous stitch ending point diagonally to the center crease folded edge and back down to the opposite edge, parallel with the starting point. Stitch along the marked line through the band only. Continue stitching the band to the scarf along the first crease line (d). Turn the band to the underside and slipstitch the folded edge to the seam-allowance stitching line (e). You may need to do some trimming, depending on the bulk of the fabric.

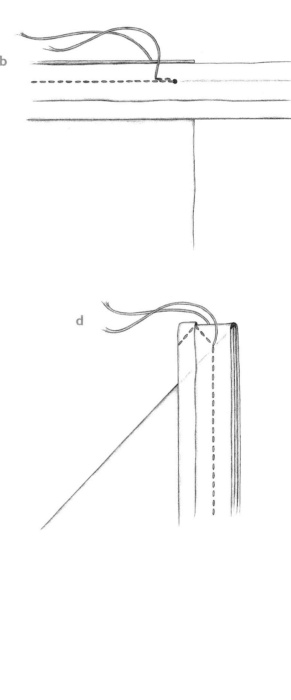

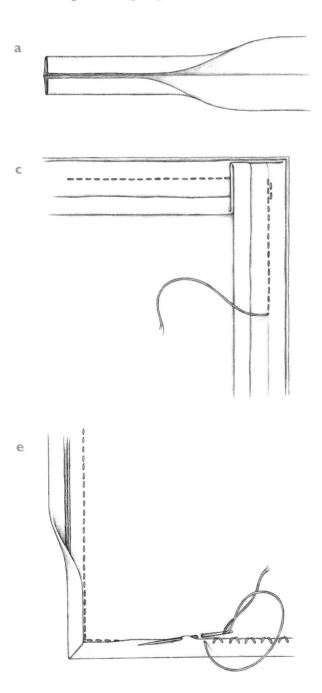

bias binding

Binding is a beautiful way to finish an edge. Bindings can blend or accent an edge. They are cut on the bias so they will lie smooth around curves and corners.

cutting bias

Using a rectangular piece of fabric, fold the fabric diagonally at one end to find the true bias. Using the bias fold as a guideline, mark parallel lines the desired width, allowing a ¼-in. seam allowance. Piecing the strips together is done in one of two ways:

continuous pieced strips—On the marked piece of fabric, join the shorter ends, right sides together, with one strip width extending beyond the edge at each side (a). Stitch a ¼-in. seam and press open (b). Begin cutting on the marked line at one end and continue in a circular fashion (c).

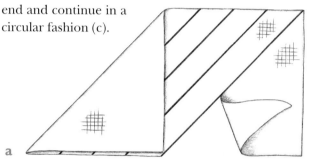

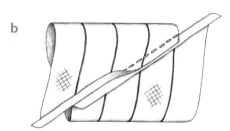

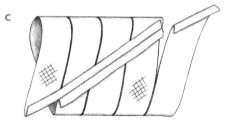

individual pieced strips—Cut along the markings for the bias strips. With right sides together, match the seamlines of the short diagonal ends and stitch (a). Press the seam open (b).

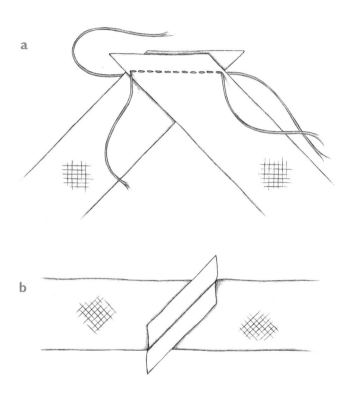

single binding

Cut bias strips four times the finished width plus ¼ in. to ⅜ in. Press in half lengthwise and press the raw edges to the center crease line. Open out and, matching raw edges, stitch along the seamline (a). Turn the bias over the seam allowance and slipstitch over the seamline (b).

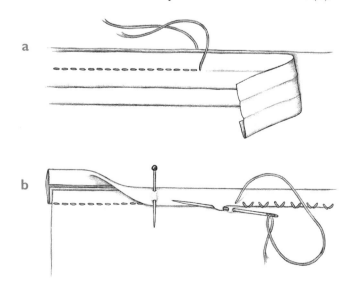

double binding (French)

Cut bias strips six times the finished width plus ¼ in. to ⅜ in. Fold in half lengthwise with wrong sides together and press. Matching raw edges, stitch the bias to the right side of the fabric along the seamline (a). Turn the strip over the seamline and slipstitch in place (b). If the bias has been cut slightly wider, the bias can be completed by machine-stitching in the well of the seam and catching the folded edge on the underside.

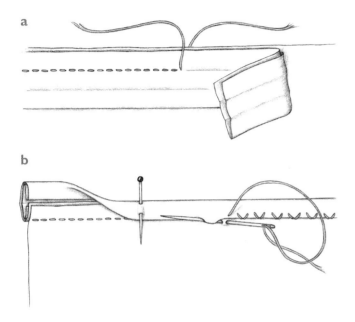

a

b

When it is necessary to change the performance of a fabric—to add weight and drape, conceal raw edges, or add an accent color or texture—lining or underlining techniques are useful.

lining

Lining gives a scarf a smooth, luxurious feeling for added comfort as well as a quality finished look. A lining prolongs the life of the piece and hides the inner construction details. It prevents stretching, helps preserve the shape, reduces wrinkling, and adds body to limp fabrics. Linings are meant to show, especially in scarves, so some thought needs to be given to the color, texture, and weight of the fabric chosen. The same fabric as the scarf top may be selected, or the fabric may be contrasting, patterned, sheer, or simply outrageous.

underlining

Underlining fabrics are cut to the same size as the outer fashion fabric pieces. Then the underlining and fashion fabric are basted and sewn together to act as one layer throughout the construction. Underlining adds body and durability by supporting and reinforcing the fabric and seams. It helps to reduce wrinkling and prevent stretching. Some underlinings alter the overall effect of the outer fabric, adding richness and visual weight. Some suggestions for underlinings include batiste, China silk, organza, muslin, taffeta, and flannel.

joining binding

A single or double binding is joined by stopping your stitching slightly before reaching an area of the joining. Open out the strip and fold the scarf so the strip ends are at right angles. Stitch the ends close to the scarf, but without catching the scarf in the stitching. Trim the seam allowances to ¼ in. and press open. Finish stitching the strip to the scarf across the joining.

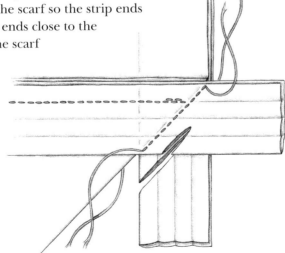

ribbon fantasy

*For carefree days and gala nights, delicately hazy sheers,
iridescent ribbons, and open-weave lattices work together
to make exciting new scarves. Learn to make gossamer scarves
to lighten a tailored suit, replenish the little black dress,
or elevate a denim ensemble.*

finished size

19 in. by 64 in.

artists

Stephanie Valley and Linda Lee

materials

- 1⅞ yd. polyester or silk chiffon
- 1⅞ yd. polyester or silk chiffon (lining)
- Silk flower bouquets (need 36 individual flower layers)
- 4 yd., ½-in.-wide variegated sheer-silk ribbon
- Cotton sewing thread
- Silk thread
- Basic sewing kit (see pp. 4-8)

cutting instructions

SCARF

Cut one 20-in. by 65-in. piece of chiffon.

LINING

Cut one 20-in. by 65-in. piece of coordinating chiffon.

ORNAMENTS

Cut two 2-yd. pieces of ribbon. Separate layers of flower petals and remove from bouquet.

floating flower

*Using two colors of sheer fabric
and delicate iridescent ribbon and flowers,
create a fresh floating cascade of soft ornamentation
on the ends of a simple scarf.*

1 Working on one layer of a chiffon length, playfully lay the ribbon onto one end of the scarf. Begin at one side edge, loop, curve, and loosely meander the ribbon through the center, and end at the opposite edge. Adjust the ribbon until you are comfortable with the overall design, and then pin (see the drawing below).

2 Using silk thread, hand-tack the ribbon in place every few inches. Position the tacks to maintain the design when the scarf is hanging.

3 Separate the petals, leaves, and stems of several purchased silk flower bouquets. Press the flower sections, if necessary.

4 Using individual flowers, layer two sections to make one "new" flower. Place approximately nine flowers on the ribbon design, spacing them in a pleasing manner. Using silk thread, hand-tack through all layers.

5 To make the flower centers, cut 1-in.-long strips of ribbon. Roll each strip into a circle and hand-tack in place (see the drawing at right).

6 Repeat steps 1 through 5 at the other end of the scarf.

7 With right sides together, pin the lining to the scarf. Stitch around all sides, leaving an opening along one side. Trim the seam to $\frac{1}{8}$ in. Turn the scarf to the outside and slipstitch the opening. Lightly press the edges.

finished size
10 in. by 60 in.

artists
Linda Lee and Stephanie Valley

materials
• 8½ yd., 1¼-in.-wide iridescent
  organdy ribbon
• Rayon decorative thread
• Brush-off or water-soluble
  stabilizer
• Assortment of seed beads
  and 20 larger beads
• Beading needle
• Silk thread
• Basic sewing kit (see pp. 4-8)

cutting instructions
Cut five 60-in. strips of organdy
ribbon.

ribbon ladder

*Rows of iridescent ribbon are sewn together
"in the air" in this magical creation. Add some luscious
beads for decoration and weight, and you have a fine
web of beautiful materials.*

1. Place the stabilizer on a blocking board or other flat surface (see the drawing below). To determine ribbon-placement lines, draw two vertical lines 1¼ in. apart (the width of the ribbon). Draw four more sets of vertical lines, allowing ¾ in. space between each pair.

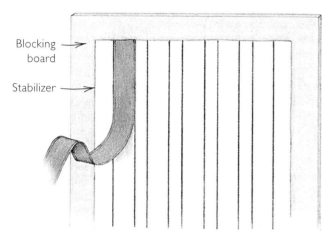

Blocking board →

Stabilizer →

2. Place the right edge of a ribbon strip on a corresponding line on the stabilizer. Using rayon decorative thread and a small stitch length (about 2mm), stitch along the finished ribbon edge.

3. Stitch along the other edge of the ribbon. Continue to stitch both sides of all five strips of ribbon.

4. Using a fine chalk marker, draw a crosswise line at the end of the scarf.

5. Starting at one side, stitch along the marked line to the opposite edge. Placing the needle in the fabric, pivot the fabric and sew seven to eight stitches (about ⅝ in.) down the side of the outer ribbon. Pivot the fabric again and sew a parallel line to the other side (see the drawing below). Sew in a continuous ladder-shaped grid the entire length of the scarf.

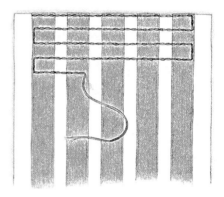

6. Using a serger, adjust the settings for a two- or three-thread roll-hem stitch formation. Serge across each end of the scarf, encasing the last row of machine stitching in the roll hem. Thread the chainstitch tails in a hand-sewing needle and feed back into the roll hem.

7. Remove the stabilizer.

8. Using silk thread and a beading needle, take one stitch at one bottom corner of one ribbon. Slip 30 seed beads and one larger bead onto a single strand of thread. Feed the needle back through the seed beads (see the drawing at right) and knot the thread at the rolled edge. Repeat at both corners of each ribbon on both ends.

Maneuvering the fabric and stabilizer from side to side in the sewing machine can be cumbersome. Try rolling each end toward the presser foot to reduce the amount of bulk to handle.

When using stabilizers, test the removal process first on a scrap of ribbon or fabric. Make sure the materials will withstand extreme heat or water.

rolled rose border

*Organdy-ribbon rosebuds are sewn to the end
of this scarf and then wired to "pouf." Choose pastels
for a summer garden party or the drama of black georgette
with red roses for a winter gala. Whatever the colors,
the effect is theatrical.*

finished size

24 in. by 72 in.

artists

Stephanie Valley and Linda Lee

materials

- 2 yd. silk georgette
- 30 yd., 1½-in.-wide variegated organdy ribbon
- Silk thread
- 2-ply cotton embroidery thread
- 20-in. 24-gauge wire
- Needlenose pliers
- Wire cutter
- Basic sewing kit (see pp. 4-8)

cutting instructions

Cut one 25-in. by 72-in. piece of silk georgette.

construction

1 Using 2-ply cotton embroidery thread, "baby-hem" each end of the scarf (see p. 11).

2 To make individual rolled roses, cut the silk ribbon into thirty ⅞-yd. lengths.

3 For each length, fold one end of the ribbon down, forming a diagonal fold (as shown below). Overlap the end ½ in.

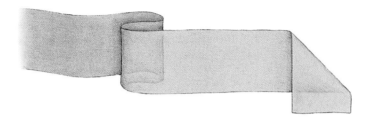

4 Fold the right edge to meet the left edge.

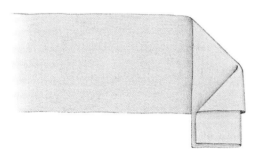

5 Starting at the right folded edge, roll the tail several times. To anchor the flower center, hand-tack through the bottom edges several times (see the drawing below). Knot the thread.

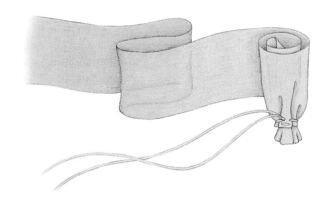

6 Using the same thread length that has been knotted, sew a running stitch along the bottom edge of the remaining ribbon.

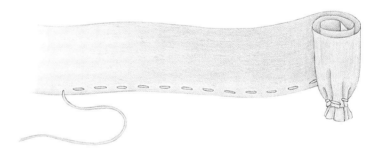

7 Pull the thread to lightly shirr the ribbon. When gathered into a flower, hand-tack the ribbon layers to hold the shape.

8 Repeat steps 3 through 7 for 30 roses.

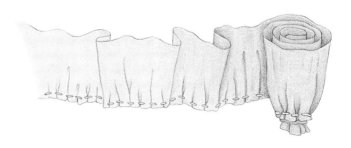

9 Cut two strips of ribbon 24 in. long. Tack 15 roses to each strip.

10 On the right side, align one edge of the ribbon with the finished scarf edge. Using silk thread and small, even stitches, hand-sew both edges of the ribbon strip to each end of the scarf (see the drawing below). Turn each ribbon end under $\frac{1}{4}$ in. to finish.

11 To form a casing, hand-sew another 24-in. piece of ribbon to the wrong side.

12 Cut two pieces of wire 10 in. long. Feed the wire through each ribbon casing, shirring the scarf onto the wire. Twist the two wire ends together and feed the ends back into the casing. Tack the scarf edges together.

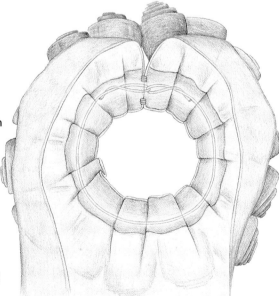

(View from inside)

finished size
16 in. by 64 in.

artist
Karen Morris

materials
• 1⅞ yd. lace
• 1⅞ yd. silk chiffon (lining)
• 4mm and 7mm silk ribbon in five or six colors
• Seed beads and larger round and square beads
• Thread
• Beading needle
• Basic sewing kit (see pp. 4-8)

fabric notes

Choose a lace with a geometric or floral design. A thick lace requires a bolder application of trim, so the trim doesn't get lost.

If you can't find ribbon in the colors you want, paint a few lengths of ribbon with textile paint, applying the paint unevenly so it looks like hand-dyed ribbon. After allowing the ribbon to air-dry, iron it with a dry iron to make the color permanent.

cutting instructions

LACE TOP
Cut one 17-in. by 65-in. piece of lace.

LINING
Cut one 17-in. by 65-in. piece of silk chiffon.

EMBELLISHMENTS
Cut 12-in. to 18-in. lengths of five or six colors of silk ribbon.

re-embroidered lace

By hand-sewing delicate ribbons and colorful beads to lace fabric, you can replicate authentic French re-embroidered lace. Line with contrasting silk chiffon to make an extraordinary scarf.

1. Take some time to plan the arrangement of the ribbon embroidery. Karen decided on an unstructured arrangement, gathering lengths of ribbon and placing them on the lace as if they are floating or being blown by the wind. Concentrate the embroidery in the lower 14 in. at each end of the scarf.

2. Working with the 12-in. to 18-in. lengths of ribbon, cut the ends on an angle to reduce raveling and machine-sew a long basting stitch close to one edge (see the drawing below). Use a thread that matches the background lace to avoid changing thread colors for each ribbon.

3. Pull the basting thread to gather each length of ribbon. Spread the gathers along the ribbon and lay it on the right side of the lace, playing with the shape until it pleases you. Use a few pins to anchor the ribbon until you can sew it in place, as shown in the drawing below.

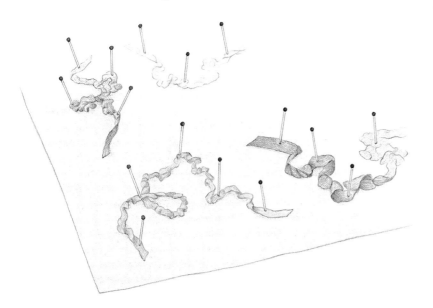

4. Working from the wrong side of the lace, delicately tack the ribbon to the lace, catching just the bottom gathered edge of the ribbon.

> *When working with a more formal design, tuck the ribbon's ends through the lace and anchor them from the back or fold the corner of each cut end under and stitch it to the lace.*

5. Select beads in a few colors to complement the lace and ribbon and scatter them along the flowing ribbon shapes to catch the light. Anchor each bead from the back side.

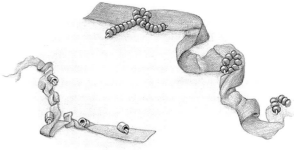

6. With right sides together, pin the lining to the embellished top. Stitch around all sides, leaving an opening along one side. Trim the corners, turn the scarf to the outside, and slipstitch the opening.

woven "rags"

Making this scarf will take you back to your childhood days of weaving pot holders on a small loom. Gather some colorful fabric, loosely weave it, add a fun button or two, and make a clever, casual scarf.

finished size
8 in. by 54 in.

artist
Bird Ross

materials
- ⅛ yd. solid-color rayon fabric (cuff)
- 1⅞ yd. solid-color silk fabric (warp strips)
- 1½ yd. print rayon fabric (weft strips)
- Two buttons
- Thread
- Basic sewing kit (see pp. 4-8)

fabric notes
You can use any fabric to weave this scarf—cotton, rayon, linen, wool, polyester, or silk. Experiment with the process to determine the "gauge" and weight of certain fabrics. There's a limit to how bulky you will want it. Both prints and solids may be combined. The scarf shown here uses the fabrics as outlined in the materials list.

cutting instructions

CUFF
Cut two 4-in. by 14-in. pieces of fabric.

WARP STRIPS
Cut or tear eighteen 1½-in.- to 2-in.-wide by 63-in.-long pieces of fabric. (The length is determined by measuring from wrist to wrist across your shoulders and adding about 3 in. The width of the strips is determined by the weight and weave of the fabric and by what sort of heft you want in your scarf. Make a test section to check.)

WEFT STRIPS
Cut or tear about thirteen 1½-in.- to 2-in.-wide by 54-in.-long pieces of fabric.

1 Twist the ends of 18 warp strips and sew them to the right side of the long edge of one cuff, evenly spacing the strips and matching raw edges (see the drawing below). Leave ½-in. seam allowances at each end of the cuff. Continue to twist the warp strips into tubular shapes and attach the other ends to the second cuff in the same manner. Twist each strip consistently so that all the strips are the same thickness.

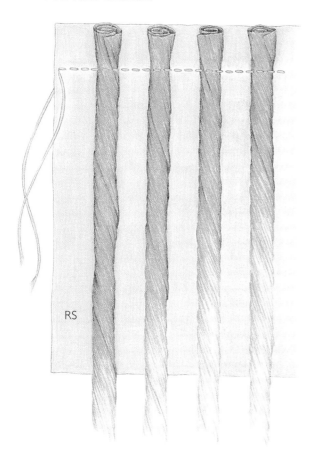

2 Tack the cuff and warp strips to a bulletin board or a wall so the strips hang vertically, or suspend in an open space such as a door jamb. To maintain consistency in the width of the scarf, draw or tape some reference marks on both sides of the warp length. Add weights to the bottom of the warp to keep the strips from twisting (clothespins work well).

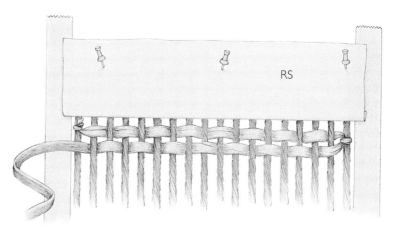

3 Working with the 13 or so weft strips, tie the first weft strip to the warp at the upper left. Weave this strip over and under the warp strips, being sure to twist the fabric as you go. At the last warp strip on the right side, tie the weft strip, reverse, and weave to the left, as shown in the drawing above. Use the reference marks to maintain a consistent width.

4 Continue weaving until you get to the end of the weft strip. Tie a second strip to the first and continue weaving. Weave and tie on until you have completed the entire warp length.

> *Don't be in a hurry when weaving. It will be time-consuming, but consistency is the goal so that the weave will be loose rather than dense. Strive to keep the weft strips about the same distance apart as the warp strips.*

5 Press each remaining long edge of the cuffs to the wrong side. With right sides together, fold each cuff in half lengthwise. Stitch the short ends, as shown in the drawing below. Trim and turn to the outside. Slipstitch the long edges together.

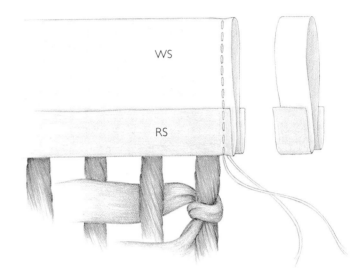

WS

RS

6 Make a crocheted button loop on one end of each cuff (see p. 9). Sew a button to the opposite end of each cuff.

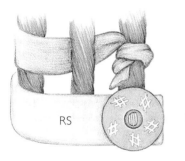

RS

> *Wear this scarf over your shoulders with your arms through the "sleeves," or wrap it around your neck a few times and use the buttons and loops to attach the scarf to itself.*

traditional arts

*Heirlooms to cherish, these scarves represent our need
to pass down the arts of piecing, appliqué, cutwork, and shadow
work to a new generation. Using the sewing machine, learn
to emulate traditional hand-sewing details while preserving
the essence of our handwork heritage.*

finished size

11 in. by 58 in.

artist

JoAnn Pugh-Gannon

materials

- 1⅔ yd. silk douppioni
- 2½ yd. wide insertion lace
- 1⅓ yd. narrow insertion lace
- 2 yd. edging lace
- Two spools #60/2 fine cotton embroidery thread
- Edgestitch foot
- 5-groove pintuck foot
- 2.5mm double needle
- Semiautomatic buttonhole foot
- Appliqué scissors
- Fade-away marker
- Spray starch
- Basic sewing kit (see pp. 4-8)

fabric notes

Because silk douppioni is a crisp silk, appropriate substitutes include Thai silk and light- and medium-weight linen and cottons. All-cotton lace insertions and lace edgings are the best.

cutting instructions

Cut one 11-in. by 58-in. piece of silk douppioni.
Cut four 20-in.- to 22-in.-long pieces of wide lace.
Cut two 20-in.- to 22-in.-long pieces of narrow lace.
Cut two 32-in.-long pieces of edging lace.

heirloom sampler

This crisp and feminine scarf introduces the art of French heirloom sewing by machine. Insert lace and entredeux into silk douppioni and create a keepsake scarf for generations to come.

1 Spray-starch and press each lace piece before using.

2 Measure and mark the center on each short end of the silk douppioni piece. Measure up 6 in. on each side and mark. Using a fade-away marker, connect the side marks with the center marks to create pointed ends. Measure up 3 in. from the marks on each side and from the center point. Mark with small dots. Using a fade-away marker, connect the side marks and center mark. Cut along the two lower lines to form the pointed ends.

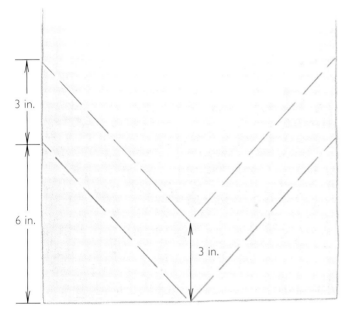

3 in.

6 in.

3 in.

3 Using a narrow, short zigzag stitch (width = 1½mm, length = 1mm) and an edgestitch foot, stitch one wide piece of lace to one narrow piece, butting the edges together. The zigzag stitch should be contained in the header of the lace. Add a second piece of wide lace to the remaining side of the narrow lace. Set this section of lace aside. Repeat this wide-narrow-wide sequence with the remaining three pieces of lace.

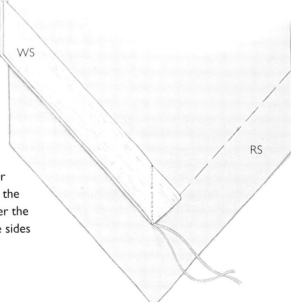

WS

RS

4 With the wrong side of the pieced lace to the right side of the silk douppioni, pin the bottom edge of the lace section to the upper marked line, ending at the center point. Fold the lace back on itself. Remove the pins and miter the lace by stitching a straight line parallel to the sides (see the drawing at right).

5 Trim the lace very close to the stitching. Press. Open out the lace and pin the mitered lace to each end of the scarf. Using the same zigzag stitch length as in step 3, sew the top and bottom edges of the lace to the silk (see the drawing at right).

6 Using appliqué scissors, carefully trim the silk from behind the lace insertions. Trim as close to the stitching as possible.

7 Using a 2.5mm double needle and a 5-groove pintuck foot, sew three rows of pintucks above each lace insertion and one row of pintucking below (as shown in the drawing below). Position the first row one presser foot width away from each side of the lace. Position the second and third row one presser foot width away from the previous row.

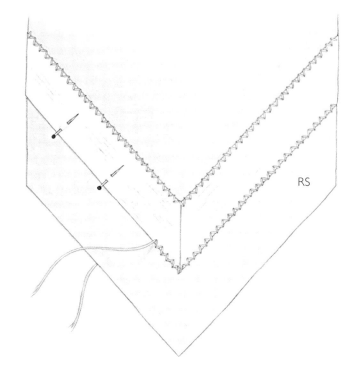

RS

8 Gather the lace edging to fit the bottom edge. There is a gathering thread in the header of the lace. Distribute the gathers evenly.

9 Pin the gathered lace edging to the bottom edge, pivoting at the point. Using an edgestitch foot and a narrow, short zigzag stitch (width = 2mm, length = 1mm), stitch the top edge of the gathered lace to the silk douppioni (see the drawing below).

10 Using a semiautomatic buttonhole foot and a narrow, short zigzag stitch (width = 3mm, length = ½mm, left needle position), roll-hem the long side edges of the scarf. Press.

cutwork linen

*This smart, summer scarf is enhanced
by a simple motif defined in cutwork. Learn to sew
perfect satin stitches with points and curves and cut away
some fabric without weakening it.*

finished size

22-in. by 32-in. by 22-in. triangle

artist

JoAnn Pugh-Gannon

materials

- 1 yd. linen
- Tagboard
- Wash-away stabilizer
- Spring hoop
- Marking pen
- #40 rayon thread
- Darning presser foot
- Embroidery presser foot
- Embroidery scissors
- Basic sewing kit (see pp. 4-8)

fabric notes

Use a closely woven fabric, such as linen, satin, or cotton.

cutting instructions

Cut one 26-in. by 37-in. by 26-in. linen triangle.

1 Using the scaled drawing below as a guide, enlarge the design to full scale on a plain piece of paper or tagboard. (The drawing is shown at 65% of actual size.)

2 Trace the cutwork design on a layer of wash-away stabilizer.

3 Starting from the bottom, layer two layers of stabilizer, the center point of the linen triangle, and the stabilizer with the design on it (see the drawing below). Insert these layers tautly in a spring hoop so that the fabric will lie flat while stitching.

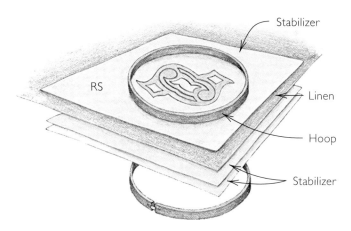

Stabilizer

RS

Linen

Hoop

Stabilizer

4 Lower the feed dogs on your sewing machine and attach a darning foot. Using a normal straight stitch, outline the design.

5 Select a narrow satin stitch (width = 1½mm to 2mm), raise the feed dogs, and attach an embroidery foot. Following the outline stitching, satin-stitch around the design, as shown below.

how to sew corners and curves

square corners

Sew to the outer corner and stop with the needle in the work at the outer corner. Turn the work and continue sewing. In this way, the corner is sewn twice and reinforced.

pointed corners

Sew to within 2mm of the corner. Continue sewing and at the same time reduce the zigzag to 0 width. Turn the work, reset the zigzag width, position the needle, and continue sewing.

blunt corners and curves

Sew until the needle is to the middle of the angle. Raising the presser foot and turning the fabric slightly, sew out from the center, replacing the needle in the middle after every stitch. Sew small curves in the same way.

6 Using small embroidery scissors, carefully trim away the linen on the innermost sections of the stitching. Cut close to the satin stitches without cutting them.

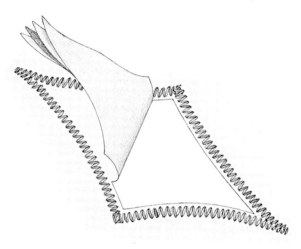

7 Wash the scarf in cool water to remove the stabilizer. Press.

8 Turn the edge allowances to the wrong side, making a finished $1/2$-in.-wide hem. Topstitch two rows of stitching on all sides, as shown below.

finished size
15 in. by 71 in.

artist
Kathy Davis

materials

- Ten 14-in. by 14-in. kimono squares in five to seven coordinating colors and motifs
- 2 yd. silk jacquard crepe de chine (lining)
- 1 yd., 6-in.-long rayon fringe
- Thread
- Graph paper
- Colored pencils
- Tagboard
- Clear ruler
- Chalk marker
- Rotary cutter and mat
- Basic sewing kit (see pp. 4-8)

fabric notes

Kimono fabrics are usually available in 14-in. widths and also in precut squares (see Resources on p. 152). When substituting regular fabric yardage, purchase 1/4-yd. to 1/2-yd. pieces of five to seven coordinating silk fabrics.

cutting instructions

Cut the kimono sections after doing steps 1 and 2 (see p. 46).

TOP

Cut about 80 pieces of mixed kimono fabrics 3 in. wide by various lengths in 1/2-in. increments ranging from 2 in. to 7 1/2 in. Use a tagboard template, chalk marker, ruler, and rotary cutter for cutting accuracy. (See steps 1 and 2 on p. 46.)

LINING

Cut one 15 1/2-in. by 72-in. piece of silk jacquard.

TRIM

Cut two 15-in. pieces of fringe.

kimono patchwork

Random lengths of mixed kimono pieces make up the surface of this oversized scarf. Finish it with a long rayon fringe and silk jacquard lining for a smashing, one-of-kind evening wrap.

① Lay out a group of fabrics in a series of different lengths, colors, and motifs to get a sense of how the fabrics work together. Look for balance in texture and color. Stand back and evaluate the "visual weight" of the pieces. Assign a colored pencil color to each different fabric and record the selections.

② On the graph paper, draw the finished size of the scarf. Divide the rectangle into five lengthwise sections each 3 in. wide. Using your color and fabric study as a guide, color in the appropriate fabrics, varying the lengths of the sections from 2 in. to 7½ in. Stagger the seams.

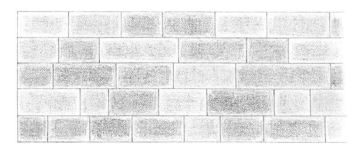

③ Cut a 3-in. by 7½-in. piece of tagboard for a template and mark in ½-in. increments. Using the colored graph as a guide, cut each kimono section.

④ With right sides together, sew the sections together end to end using a ¼-in. seam (see the drawing below). Press the seams open. Sew one lengthwise strip at a time, completing a total of five strips.

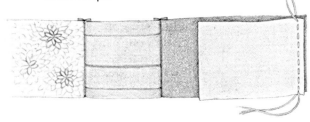

⑤ With right sides together, sew the lengthwise strips together using ¼-in. seams. Press the seams open.

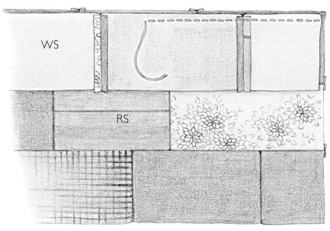

⑥ Position the bound edge of the rayon fringe along each short end of the pieced scarf. Baste in place, as shown in the drawing below. Tape the fringe together to avoid catching it in the seams.

⑦ With rights sides together, sew the lining to the pieced scarf, leaving an opening. Turn the scarf to the outside and slipstitch the opening.

sari wrap

*This sensational double-layer and banded-silk
scarf is trimmed with silk and metallic embroidered ribbon
that's embellished with bobbin-worked decorative threads.
A secret pocket in the lining eliminates
the need for a purse.*

finished size
14½ in. by 90 in.

artist
Jane Conlon

materials
- 2½ yd. silk douppioni
- ½ yd., 45-in.-wide contrasting silk douppioni
- 6 yd., 1-in.- to 2-in.-wide embroidered ribbon
- Seven cast-metal medallions
- One covered or matching button (match the contrasting silk douppioni)
- Disappearing marking pen
- 100% cotton thread
- Decorative threads (Pearl Crown rayon, metallics, Glamour, silk buttonhole twist)
- Hand-sewing needle
- Machine-sewing needles (sharps for sewing, embroidery needle and needle for metallic thread for bobbin work)
- Edgestitch foot
- Basic sewing kit (see pp. 4-8)

fabric notes
Any medium-weight, crisp silk may be substituted for the douppioni. Choose one color for the body of the scarf, another color for the contrasting border.

cutting instructions

BODY
Cut one 14-in. by 89½-in. piece of silk douppioni.

LINING
Cut one 14-in. by 89½-in. piece of silk douppioni.

POCKET
Cut one 3-in. by 7-in. piece of silk douppioni (welt).
Cut two 8½-in. by 9-in. pieces of silk douppioni (pocket bags).

BORDER
Cut five 2½-in. by 45-in. strips of contrasting silk douppioni on the crossgrain.

1 At 8½ in. from one end, mark and center a 1-in. by 6-in. rectangle on the right side of the scarf lining (see the drawing at right). Using the markings as the placement, construct a single-welt pocket at the end of one scarf body piece (see the sidebar on p. 50).

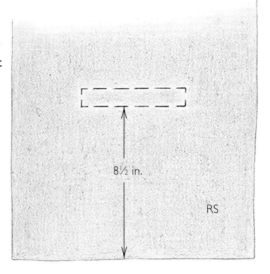

8½ in.

RS

2 Embellish one selvage edge of embroidered ribbon with parallel rows of bobbin-worked straight stitching (see the sidebar on p. 51).

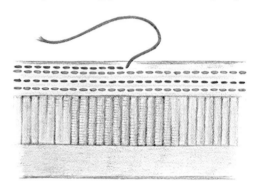

3 Place the ribbon on the outside edges of the scarf body (the piece that does not have the pocket). Determine the amount of ribbon width that will be exposed after the border has been applied. Edgestitch or hand-sew the inner edge (a). Fold the ribbon back on itself, then diagonally to the side, making a right angle. Press. Fold the band back on itself again and stitch on the diagonal crease—through the ribbon and scarf (b). If the trim is bulky, trim the excess ribbon. Press flat from the right side to form the miter and continue through all corners (c). Baste the outer edge of the ribbon to the scarf.

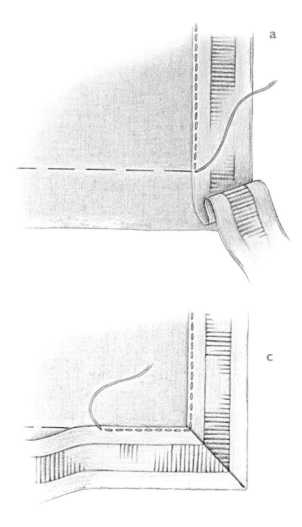

a

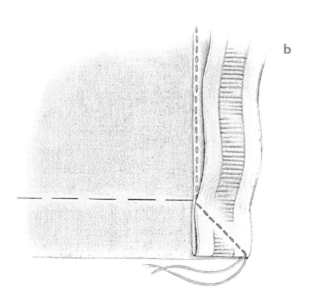

b

c

how to make a single-welt pocket

1 With wrong sides together, fold the welt in half lengthwise and press. Baste the long raw edges together using a ½-in. seam.

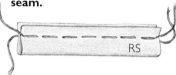

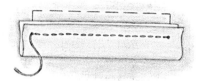

2 On the right side of the scarf body, position the basting line of the welt over the bottom placement line of the rectangle (see step 1 on p. 48). Baste to the body on top of the previous basting. Begin and end the stitching at the end markings.

3 With right sides together and matching raw edges, position one pocket bag over the welt. From the wrong side, stitch over the previous basting line, back-stitching at each end.

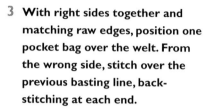

4 With right sides together, butt the short raw edge of the second pocket bag to the raw edges of the welt/pocket bag. Stitching through both layers, stitch exactly 1 in. from the previous stitching, stopping two or three stitches from the end markings.

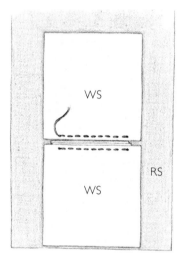

5 Slash the opening through the scarf to within ½ in. of the ends. Clip diagonally to the ends of the stitching.

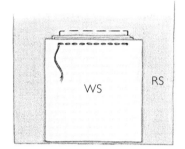

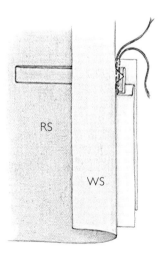

6 Turn the pocket bags to the inside of the scarf, allowing the welt to fill the opening. Fold back the scarf and stitch across the ends of the welt, catching the triangle (see the drawing at left).

7 Edgestitch across the bottom of the welt opening through all layers.

8 Sew the sides and bottom of the pocket bags together.

9 Edgestitch the remaining sides and top of the welt opening through the body and one pocket-bag layer only.

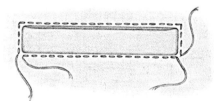

4 With wrong sides together, baste the outer edges of both scarf pieces (the body and the lining) together.

5 Make one continuous band of contrasting douppioni by sewing the 45-in. strips of fabric together with ¼-in. seams and pressing the seams open. Apply a border to all sides of the scarf, mitering four corners (see p. 17).

6 Using a heavy decorative thread, prick-stitch along the inside edge of the band (see p. 10).

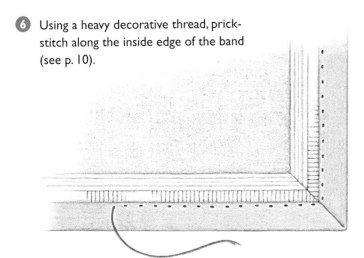

7 Evenly space three decorative cast medallions across each end and sew in place. Attach one medallion on the right band of the right side of the scarf 14 in. from the end opposite the pocket. On the same band and side, sew a covered or matching button 18 in. from the other end. On the wrong side of the scarf and behind the medallion, hand-sew a chainstitch to use as a button loop in the well of the band seam (see p. 9).

all about bobbin work

Beautiful threads such as rayon, metallic, or cotton embroidery that are too heavy to use in the needle of a conventional sewing machine can still be incorporated into a design when fed through the bobbin. Bobbin work is particularly effective when used in bands and borders.

To use a heavy thread in the bobbin, you need to loosen the bobbin tension so that the thickness of the thread is accommodated and the thread feeds evenly. Loosen the tension screw on the bobbin case. Using a small screwdriver, carefully turn the screw to the left until the desired tension is achieved—usually no more than a quarter of a turn.

Wind heavy thread onto the bobbin slowly, either by hand or machine. Don't overfill.

Bobbin work is done by sewing with the wrong side of the scarf up using an embroidery or topstitching needle. An edgestitch foot aids in keeping the stitching lines parallel. When a row of stitching is complete, lift the presser foot and cut the thread, leaving a thread tail. Pull on the lighter thread from the wrong side of the fabric (the side you have sewn on), and it will draw the top thread through. Knot on the wrong side of the garment.

Paint and antique the cast-metal medallions to coordinate with your fabrics.

finished size
12 in. by 90 in.

artist
JoAnn Pugh-Gannon

materials

- ¼ yd. white China silk
- ¼ yd. pastel China silk
- Tagboard
- Marking pen
- Silk basting thread
- Open embroidery foot
- Semiautomatic buttonhole foot
- #60/2 cotton embroidery thread
- Basic sewing kit (see pp. 4-8)

fabric notes

Shadow work can be sewn on any transparent or semitransparent fabric such as cotton lawn, voile, batiste, handkerchief linen, or fine silks.

cutting instructions

Cut two 12½-in. by 45-in. (the width of the fabric) pieces of white China silk.
Cut two 12½-in. by 9-in. pieces of pastel China silk.

shadow-work silk

Shadow work or shadow appliqué is a delicate technique worked in fine transparent or semitransparent fabric with a solid color stitched to the underneath to "shadow" through. Embellish a scarf with this technique or use it on the yoke of a blouse or dress, on exquisite sleepwear, or on children's wear.

1 With right sides together, sew the short ends of the white China silk together. Overstitch the straight stitch with a very narrow zigzag. Trim close to the stitching.

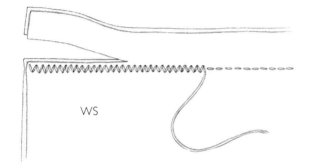

WS

2 Using the scaled drawing below as a guide, enlarge the edge design to full scale on plain paper or tagboard.

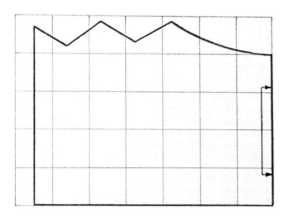

I square = I in.

3 Trace the design across the width of each piece of pastel China silk, using a marking pen. Cut along the design line.

4 Pin one piece of pastel silk under each end of the white silk, aligning the straight ends. Baste the ends together and along the decorative edge.

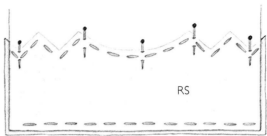

RS

5 Using an open embroidery foot, fine cotton (60/2) embroidery thread, and a narrow, short zigzag or pin stitch (width = 1mm, length = ½mm), stitch on the white China silk side along the raw edge of the pink underlay. One side of this stitch should fall into the white silk and the other into the pink. Press.

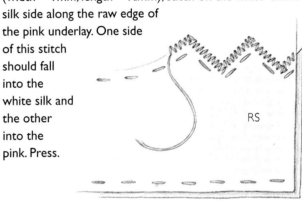

RS

6 Select a decorative stitch. Stitch across the width of the scarf about 2 in. from each end.

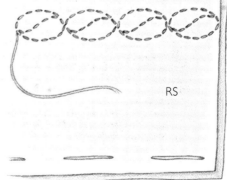

RS

7 Using a semiautomatic buttonhole foot, roll-hem all edges with a narrow, short zigzag stitch (width = 3mm, length = 1mm, left needle position). Press.

finished size
24 in. by 68 in.

artist
Kathy Davis

materials

- 1¾ yd. solid-color silk crepe de chine
- 2 yd. silk jacquard
- Ten 14-in. by 14-in. squares of kimono fabric
- Four small tassels
- Thread
- Tagboard
- Marking pen
- Clear ruler
- Rotary cutter and mat
- Basic sewing kit (see pp. 4-8)

fabric notes

See Resources on p. 152 for a listing of where to purchase kimono sample packs. Silk douppioni or other fairly crisp silks can be substituted for kimono squares. You'll need ¼ yd. of 8 to 10 different fabrics for the obi appliqués and the border.

cutting instructions

BACKGROUND
Cut one 21-in. by 64½-in. piece of silk crepe de chine.

LINING
Cut one 25-in. by 68½-in. piece of silk jacquard.

BORDER
Cut 10 colors of kimono fabrics into 2½ in. wide strips.

OBI APPLIQUÉS
See step 1 (p. 56) for details on preparing the appliqués.

obi appliqué

Delightful appliqués reminiscent of Japanese obi sash knots embellish this large scarf/wrap. A traditional pieced border, which also uses kimono fabrics, outlines this unique accessory.

1 Enlarge the scaled drawing at right and make tagboard templates for each part of the obi appliqués. Add ¼-in. seam allowances to each template. Each obi appliqué has four parts and uses two fabrics, one dark and one light in value. Mix the fabrics for interest and cut enough pieces to make eight obi appliqués. Cut each section of the obi appliqué on the same grain as it will lie on the background.

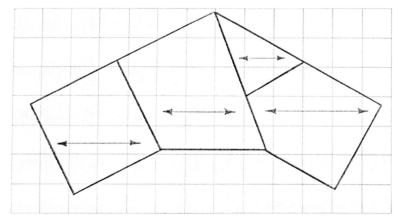

1 square = 1 in.

2 With right sides together, sew the four sections together for each obi appliqué. Press the seam allowances open.

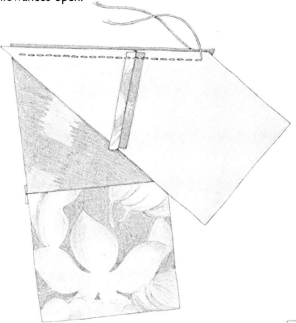

The obi appliqués may be sewn on by machine using either a satin stitch or blanket stitch.

3 Cut a 1½-in. by 9-in. rectangle of tagboard. Draw a line ¼ in. from one long edge. Place the template ¼ in. from a raw edge on the wrong side of the obi appliqué. Press a ¼-in. seam allowance up and over the edge of the template. Press all raw edges of each obi appliqué to the wrong side using this method.

4 Following the scaled layout below, pin the obi appliqués to the silk background. Slipstitch each section in place.

1 square = 2 in.

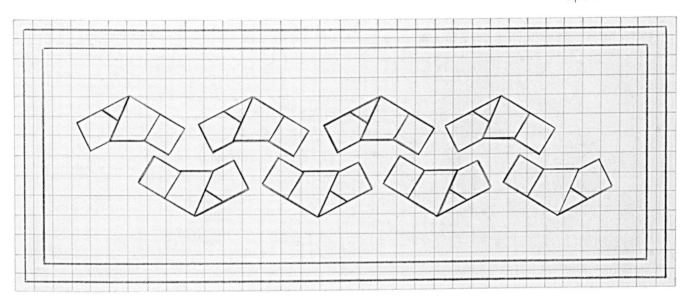

5 With right sides together, sew the 2½-in.-wide fabric strips together, using a ¼-in. seam allowance. Press the seams open. Using a clear ruler and a rotary cutter, cut 2½-in.-wide strips perpendicular to the seams. Sew these strips together end to end, creating a long pieced border.

6 With right sides together, sew the pieced border to all sides of the background. Press the seams open.

7 With the tassel fringe to the inside, baste one tassel cord to each corner of the background.

8 With right sides together, sew the lining to the background, leaving a 6-in. opening. Trim the corners. Turn to the outside and slipstitch the opening.

contemporary interpretations

Do not fold, bend, or mutilate—except in the case of these scarves. Let these innovative designers show you how to slash, wash, shrink, etch, and fuse your way into making the most interesting scarves. You'll question the process, but love the results. Surprise!

finished size

approximately 12 in. by 86 in.

artist

Karen Morris

materials

- 1 yd. Ultrasuede Light
- Rotary cutter with decorative blade
- Leather punch tool (see Resources on p. 152)
- Scraps of wool melton
- Chalk pencil
- Basic sewing kit (see pp. 4-8)

cutting instructions

See step 1 on the facing page for directions on cutting out the scarf.

punched Ultrasuede

Because the cut edges of Ultrasuede Light
don't ravel, this unique fabric lends itself to all
sorts of interesting techniques–in this case, fancy cut edges
and lacy punched designs on a fluid, wonderfully warm,
no-sew scarf. Make one to coordinate with your favorite
coat and find that you reach for it every day.
Or make one as a stunning gift.

1 Enlarge the scaled drawing at right and make a full-sized paper pattern of the scarf. (If you prefer, use your own design.) Using a chalk pencil, trace around the paper pattern onto Ultrasuede Light. To produce the interesting edges, cut the scarf shape using a rotary cutter with a decorative blade (I used a curvy Victorian blade from Fiskars). Ultrasuede Light is a nonwoven fabric so you can cut it out without regard to straight of grain.

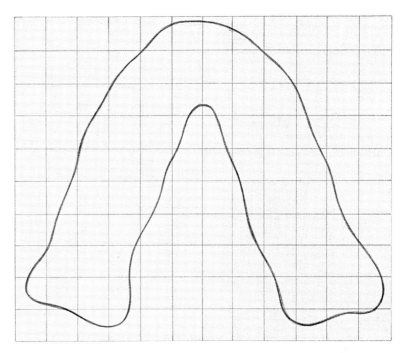

I square = I in.

2 To punch the holes in the scarf, you'll need a rotary leather punch tool. Each tool punches six holes ranging in size from $5/64$ in. to $3/16$ in. in diameter. To create a decorative border, punch holes along the cut edges in a pattern sequence of your choice. To emulate the sample scarf border motif, punch medium-sized holes close to the edge at every scallop, punch smaller holes farther from the edge and between each medium hole, and punch large holes even farther to the inside and aligned with every fifth medium hole (see below).

It's easier to get a clean hole in the Ultrasuede Light if you place a layer of dense wool melton (scraps from a leftover project) behind the scarf and punch the tool through both layers.

Try wearing this comfortable, nontraditional shape with the ends hanging loose like lapels or tied once in the front, or with one or both ends flung over the opposite shoulder.

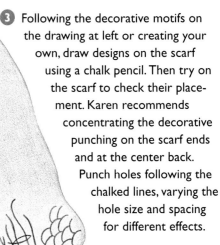

3 Following the decorative motifs on the drawing at left or creating your own, draw designs on the scarf using a chalk pencil. Then try on the scarf to check their placement. Karen recommends concentrating the decorative punching on the scarf ends and at the center back. Punch holes following the chalked lines, varying the hole size and spacing for different effects.

finished size
11 in. by 55 in.

artist
Karen Morris

materials
• 1⅝ yd. rayon/silk velvet
• 1⅝ yd. silk chiffon (lining)
• Fiber-Etch fabric remover
• Small paint brush
• A few seed beads (optional)
• Silk thread (any color)
• Basic sewing kit (see pp. 4-8)

fabric notes
Drapey rayon/silk velvets that are
approximately 82% rayon faced and
18% silk backed are recommended.
Cotton velvet is not appropriate.
Fiber-Etch removes only cellulose
fibers, so make sure the pile (or nap)
is rayon.

cutting instructions

SCARF
Cut one 12-in. by 56-in. piece
of rayon/silk velvet.

LINING
Cut one 12-in. by 56-in. piece
of silk chiffon.

dévoré velvet

The word dévoré *(French for "devoured")
aptly describes the burn-out process that produces
this rich fabric. On velvets with a silk backing and rayon
pile, a chemical solution eats away the velvet's pile in areas
where it's applied, leaving the sheer-silk backing intact.
Lined with silk chiffon, this simple but luxurious
scarf is a real work of art.*

construction

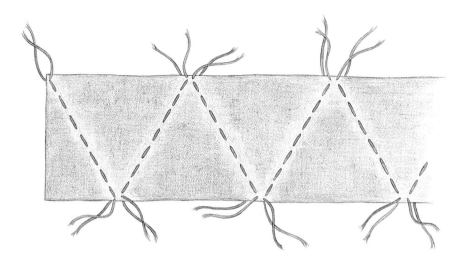

1 Starting in one corner, sew a large zigzag design across the velvet fabric with long (6mm) basting stitches, stopping as you reach each edge (see the drawing at right). After tying off one end of each "zig," pull the thread to gather and tie off the other end. Repeat for all the stitching.

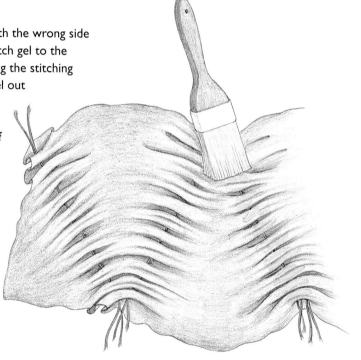

2 Lay the fabric flat with the wrong side up, apply the Fiber-Etch gel to the brush, and paint along the stitching lines, brushing the gel out onto the tops of all the curves and folds between the rows of stitching (see the drawing at right).

Although the Fiber-Etch gel product is easy and convenient to use, you may want to wear rubber gloves to protect your skin from irritation. Also, the pile dust can be irritating to breathe, so wear a mask if you're sensitive. If the gel gets on clothing or skin, just wash it off with soap and water.

3 Remove the basting threads. Using a dry iron at a silk/wool setting and a thin press cloth on the wrong side of the fabric, iron the velvet (washing and drying the fabric will fluff up any crushed pile). The manufacturer's instructions suggest using a clothes dryer for the heat stage on velvet to avoid crushing the pile, but your dryer may not be hot enough to produce the necessary chemical reaction.

It's a good idea to start by doodling on samples with the gel to see what effects you like and to learn exactly how much gel and heat are needed to remove the pile cleanly. You may end up with uneven results if you don't experiment first.

4 After ironing, scratch the pile with a fingernail to see whether it's ready to fall out. The flat side of a credit card, a toothbrush, or a flat, plastic spatula is perfect for gently scraping away the pile. While it's true that rinsing will remove the burnt-out pile, it also removes any remaining dried gel. So be sure your design has come out cleanly before rinsing. If it hasn't, iron a little more, and then scrape again.

Be careful, though. Don't let the iron get too hot or hold it too long in place because the dried gel may burn, especially in spots where it's thick. Burned gel can cause holes in the silk backing.

5 Wash the burnt-out velvet in lukewarm water in the washing machine and dry in the dryer on a moderate setting.

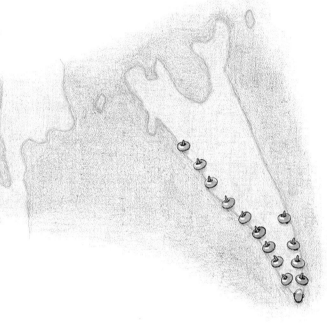

6 If you want to add an optional accent to highlight the designs on the scarf, sew a few seed beads along some of the outlines of the burnt-out areas at each end of the velvet (as shown in the drawing at right).

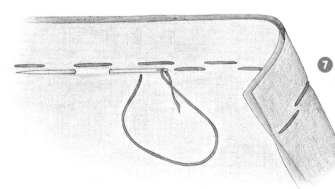

7 With right sides together, pin the lining to the velvet. Using silk thread, hand-sew double basting stitches along all edges (see the drawing at left). Basting the seams will prevent fabric creep and puckering when sewing a pile fabric to a smooth-surfaced fabric. Basting will take extra time, but the velvet is almost impossible to sew without it.

8 Loosen the tension slightly, lengthen the stitch length, and machine-sew near the basting line, leaving an opening for turning. Using a walking foot, sew with the velvet on top and hold the fabric taut in front and back of the needle. Trim the corners and press the seams open. Turn to the outside and slipstitch the opening.

To avoid crushing the velvet pile, press the velvet over any one of several pressing aids—a needle board, a bristled press cloth, or a Turkish towel. Another piece of velvet works, too.

finished size

13 in. by 66 in.

artist

Stephanie Valley

materials

- 1⅞ yd. silk georgette (scarf)
- ¼ yd. silk charmeuse (leaves)
- 1 yd. Wonder-Under fusible bonding web
- Press cloth
- Small craft scissors
- Iron
- Silk or rayon thread
- Serger
- Basic sewing kit (see pp. 4-8)

fabric notes

Polyester georgette or chiffon can be substituted for silk georgette or chiffon. The scarf fabric should be drapey, fluid, and transparent.

cutting instructions

Cut or tear (for better straight of grain) one 14-in. by 67-in. silk georgette rectangle.

laminated leaves

*This airy sheer scarf beautifully drapes
and shimmers with the addition of magical little silk
charmeuse "holes." Make it in white or luscious colors with
monochromatic or contrasting leaves.
Make your own shapes, too.*

construction

1 Set up the serger with a three-thread roll-hem stitch formation. Using silk or rayon thread, roll-hem all edges of the scarf.

2 Following the manufacturer's instructions, fuse the rough side of Wonder-Under to the entire piece of silk charmeuse. Using the template shown at right, cut approximately 100 leaf shapes in the silk charmeuse. The Wonder-Under prevents the charmeuse from raveling.

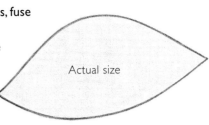

Actual size

3 On the right side of each end of the scarf, arrange a row of approximately 10 leaves, as shown in the drawing at right. Remove the paper backing from the Wonder-Under. Using a press cloth, fuse the leaves in place. Check the manufacturer's instructions for the appropriate iron setting.

4 Using small craft scissors, cut small leaf-shaped holes through the centers of the laminated leaves. Cut through both layers of fabric.

5 Randomly space the remaining leaves on the right side of the scarf and fuse in place.

6 Cut small leaf-shaped holes through some of the laminated leaves. Or cut through all of the leaves. There are no rules here—your choice.

finished size

10 in. by 60 in.

artist

Jean Williams Cacicedo

materials

- 3 yd. wool jersey (will yield four scarves)
- 12-in. by 12-in. piece of heavy paper (a manila file folder works great)
- Small (28mm) rotary cutter and cutting mat
- Large rotary cutter with "wavy" blade
- X-Acto knife or straight rotary cutter
- Basic sewing kit (see pp. 4-8)

fabric notes

The wool jersey must be 100% wool. No blends!

cutting instructions

Wool jersey shrinks nearly in half in length during the washing process. Because of the shrinkage, the actual cutting of the finished scarf is the last step. Three yards of wool jersey will yield four scarves, but one scarf also requires 3 yd. (so don't purchase less yardage).

slashed and felted

Wool jersey makes a beautiful scarf just on its own, but when it's slashed, cut, washed, and seemingly destroyed, it makes a luxuriously warm but creatively innovative scarf.

1 With wrong sides together, fold the 3-yd. piece of wool jersey in half lengthwise. Overlock or zigzag the selvages together.

2 Fold the doubled fabric in half lengthwise and cross-wise so that there are eight layers.

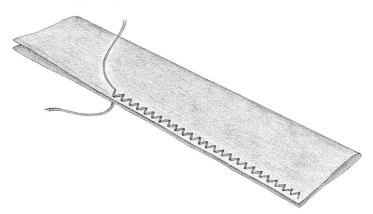

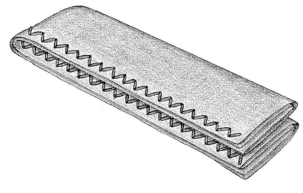

3 Using the scaled diagram shown below, draw the cutwork design on the 12-in. by 12-in. template paper (a). Following the repeat diagram, cut away ¼-in. by 1-in. rectangles with an X-Acto knife (b).

a

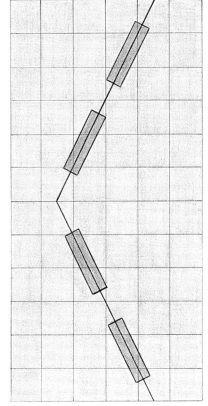

1 square = ½ in.

b

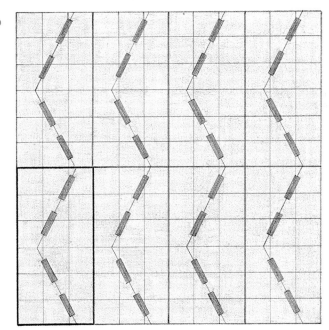

1 square = 1 in.

④ Beginning at the folded end, place the template over all eight layers of wool jersey. Use the small rotary cutter to cut through each 1/4-in. by 1-in. rectangle. A lot of pressure is required to cut through eight layers. If you have trouble, omit the last fold and cut through only four layers. Make your cuts only within the template, pressing hard. After completing all cuts in one template, move the template and repeat the design until you reach the ends, leaving about 6 in. extra fabric at the bottom.

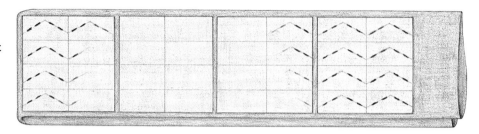

⑤ Wash the fabric in the washing machine. Use a small-load level of hot water without soap, regular agitation, and a cold rinse.

⑥ Place in the dryer, on hot, until the fabric is dry. The cut holes close up slightly and become ragged. There is no unraveling.

⑦ Cut away the overlocked edges with scissors.

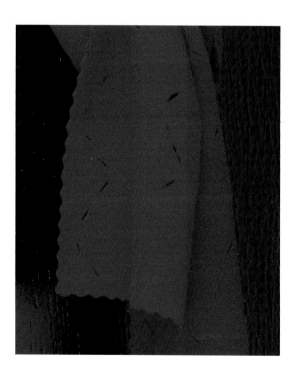

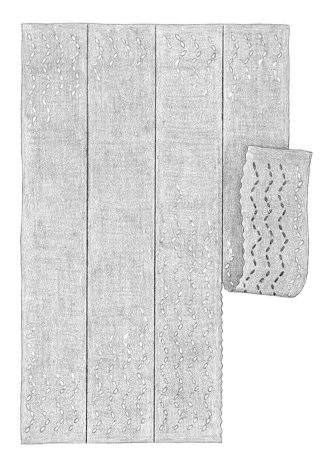

⑧ Using the wavy blade, trim all edges to make four equal rectangles.

fringed wool crepe

*Washing and drying wool crepe
is an interesting way to alter its original texture.
When it is cut into a unique shape and embellished with
washed-wool appliqués, you have a special scarf
for more than just special occasions.*

finished size
16½ in. by 54 in.

artist
Jean Williams Cacicedo

materials
- 1½ yd. wool crepe (will yield two scarves)
- ¼ yd. wool jersey or lightweight felt for appliqués
- Pinking shears
- Basic sewing kit (see pp. 4-8)

fabric notes
Make sure to use 100% wool crepe and wool jersey. Blends will not produce the same results.

cutting instructions
Cut one 54-in. by 54-in. square of wool crepe.

1. Draw a diagonal line from corner to corner on the wool-crepe square. Following the scaled drawing at right, cut along the diagonal line and cut the scarf shape.

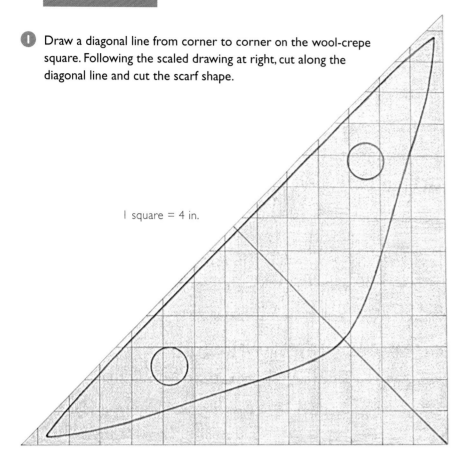

1 square = 4 in.

2. Machine-wash the wool crepe and wool jersey in hot water without soap, rinse in cold water, and dry in the dryer. (The wool crepe and wool jersey may be washed together, although sometimes the dye in the crepe will interfere with the jersey color. If you are unsure, wash test samples or wash separately.)

3. Cut two 4½-in.-diameter circles and four 1¼-in.-diameter circles in the wool jersey.

4. Pin one large wool-jersey circle about 18 in. from one end of the scarf and centered. Pin the other large wool-jersey circle on the other side of the scarf so that the wool crepe is sandwiched between the two circles (see below).

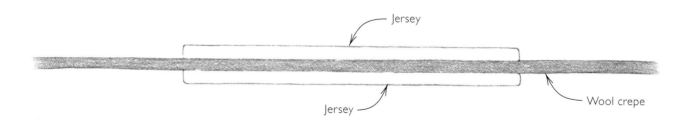

Jersey

Jersey

Wool crepe

5 Sewing through all layers, stitch four elongated ovals in X-shaped patterns ending ¼ in. from each edge.

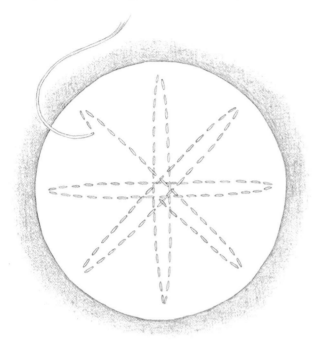

6 With regular scissors, clip from the edge of the circle to the centers between the stitching. Then trim with the pinking shears, creating a snowflake design.

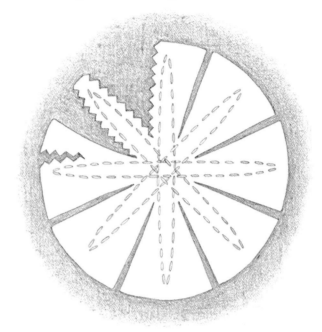

7 Place the small wool-crepe circles about 7 in. from each end and slightly off center in the same sandwich manner. Stitch two single-line and crisscrossing X designs on each circle. Clip and pink as for the large circle.

8 Press the scarf well. Washing the wool crepe will have fringed the raw edges of the scarf. Simply trim the fringe equally on all sides to finish.

beads and baubles

Everyone loves a bead or two. Whet your appetite
with a beaded border from elegant to funky, simply edged
to lacy and racy. There's even one that doesn't have a single bead
sewn on it—but wait a minute, isn't the whole scarf shaped
like a bead? Check it out.

finished size
45 in. square

artist
Jane Conlon

materials

- 1 ¼ yd. lightweight silk chiffon
  (purchase ⅛ yd. to ¼ yd. extra
  for practice samples)
- 2mm hemming foot
- Metallic, rayon, or 60-wt. cotton
  thread
- Fabric glue stick
- Size 80 machine sewing needle
  for metallic thread or machine
  embroidery needle
- Seed beads
- Large decorative beads for
  corners: crystals, gemstone beads,
  decorative metallic beads, etc.
- Nymo beading thread (lightweight)
  or 100% polyester thread
- Beeswax
- Beading needle (size appropriate
  for beads used)
- Basic sewing kit (see pp. 4-8)

fabric notes

Other transparent sheer fabrics
such as silk georgette or polyester
varieties of chiffon and georgette
may be substituted for silk chiffon.
Any choice should be lightweight
and extremely drapey.

cutting instructions

Tear or pull thread to cut one
45-in. square of silk chiffon.
Remove the selvage to prevent
the tighter threads distorting
the hemmed edge.
Fold corner to corner to check
that the dimensions are perfectly
square and, if necessary, true the
square prior to hemming.

bead-embellished hem

*Learn to trim an exquisite sheer scarf using a
standard hemming foot, a zigzag stitch, decorative metallic
thread, and small beads. Put this method into your
repertoire of finishing techniques for scarves, garment edges,
and home-decorating projects.*

1 Set up the machine for a rolled-hem stitch. Wind the bobbin and thread the needle with metallic, rayon, or 60-wt. cotton thread. Insert a needle for metallic thread or another machine embroidery needle, attach a hemming foot, and select a zigzag stitch. Jane recommends a 3mm width and a 2mm length. If you haven't used a hemming foot before, practice first on fabric scraps.

---

getting the hem started

1 Use a fabric glue stick to turn in a $\frac{1}{8}$-in. hem that extends approximately $\frac{1}{2}$ in. from the corner.

2 Place the fabric under the hemming foot and sink the needle. Grab the thread tails and hold while advancing the fabric several stitches until the corner has completely cleared the hole in the needle plate.

3 Sink the needle, raise the hemming foot, and gently lift the edge of the fabric into the scroll of the foot.

4 Lower the hemming foot and continue sewing. The foot will roll the hem, but it is up to you to ensure continuous, even feeding. For best results, use the inside of the right hemming foot toe as a guide and lift the fabric vertically as it feeds into the foot, as opposed to holding it at an angle.

---

2 Hem the raw edges of the scarf in sequence. To reduce thread breakage, sew at half-speed. If the thread does break, remove fabric from beneath the hemming foot, clip threads close to the last stitch sequence, reposition the edge beneath the foot, and continue sewing. Thread breakage should not be a problem if the correct needle is used. A dot of Sewers Aid in the eye of the needle helps reduce friction and may reduce thread breakage and facilitate even feeding of the needle thread.

3 Neaten the corners with a few hand stitches, if necessary. Press the hemmed edges prior to beading.

4 With Nymo or 100% polyester thread and a beading needle, use a running stitch worked directly through the rolled hem of the scarf to attach accent beads one by one (see the drawing below).

Bring the needle through the inside edge of the rolled hem, approximately $\frac{5}{8}$ in. from any corner of the scarf. Pick up a single bead and insert the needle into the rolled hem one bead width away. Take a stitch of $\frac{1}{2}$ in. to $\frac{5}{8}$ in. and draw the needle through the rolled hem. Add one bead per stitch, spacing the beads at regular intervals and working away from you. Knot off and add new thread lengths as necessary, hiding tail ends inside the rolled hem.

5 Add additional embellishments at each corner. Prior to sewing, stack beads onto a beading needle to determine a pleasing sequence. Once the beading sequence has been determined, knot a length of thread (double if using polyester) and bring through the hem at the scarf corner. Take a tiny stitch through all layers of fabric and add beads to the thread in the predetermined sequence. At the end of the bead sequence, pick up a seed bead, and reroute the thread through the beads.

6 Draw the thread tight to align the beads and bring the needle through the rolled hem to the right side of the scarf. Take several stitches through all layers to secure the weight of the beads and tie off, hiding the thread ends in the rolled hem.

If desired, additional strands can be added at regular intervals to either side of the corners to create a fringe effect.

knotted beads

*A series of knotted fabric buttons and beads
create dramatic tassels to adorn the ends of a sumptuous
velvet "poufed" scarf.*

finished size
7½ in. by 71 in.

artist
Diane Ericson

materials
- 1⅝ yd. stretch velour
  or rayon/silk velvet
- ⅓ yd. lightweight textured fabric
- ¼ yd. printed velvet
- ⅓ yd. silk organza
- 1½ yd. of ¼-in.-wide ribbon
  (any color) or twill tape
- ¼ yd. satin ribbon or rayon
  seam tape
- Polyester thread
- Large clean nail
- Carpet warp or buttonhole twist
- Hand sewing needle
- Fabric glue
- Basic sewing kit (see pp. 4-8)

fabric notes
The fabrics that are used in the
beaded tassels can be made up in
any combination of fabrics—rayon,
silk, or velvet in prints, solids, and
textured. Make them colorful or
monochromatic, elegant or funky.

cutting instructions

SCARF
Cut one 13-in. by 56-in. piece of
stretch velour or velvet.
Cut one 50-in.-long piece of ribbon
or twill tape.

KNOTS
Cut two 8-in. by 14-in. pieces of textured fabric (for the largest knots).
Cut two 6-in. by 12-in. pieces of
printed velvet (for the medium-sized
knots).
Cut two 4-in. by 10-in. pieces of textured fabric (for the smallest knots).

TASSELS
Cut two 12-in. by 12-in. pieces of silk
organza.
Cut two 3-in. pieces of satin ribbon
or rayon seam tape.

1 With the wrong side of the velvet up, pin the twill tape to the center of each short end. The twill tape has been cut 6 in. shorter than the fabric, so the fabric will not lie flat.

2 With right sides together, fold the velvet in half lengthwise. Sew across each end and along the length, leaving an opening. Trim the corners and turn to the right side.

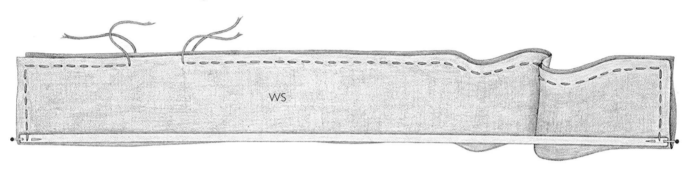

WS

3 Make six fabric knots—two large, two medium, and two small (see the sidebar on p. 82).

4 To make a tassel, place one small fabric knot in each piece of organza. Using a sharp needle and carpet warp or strong buttonhole twist, secure (knot) the thread, and sew through the knot and the center of the fabric.

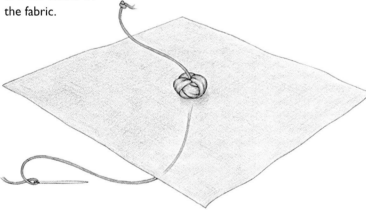

5 Draw the fabric around the knot. Using a regular needle and polyester thread, sew through the fabric, back and forth, to pleat and gather the fabric just below the knot.

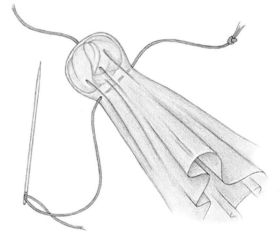

6 Wrap a 3-in. piece of satin ribbon around the base of the tassel a few times to hide the stitches. Fold the end of the ribbon under and whipstitch in place. Arrange the tassel fabric in a pleasing manner.

7 Slide one medium knot and one large knot onto each strand of strong thread at the top of the tassel.

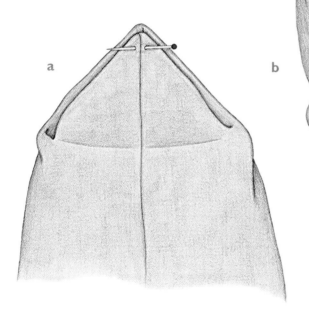

a

b

8 Bring the raw edges of the scarf ends together and pin (a). Working through the center opening of the scarf, attach the knotted tassel through all layers of the scarf fabric to secure the tassel and close both ends of the scarf (b). Knot repeatedly for extra stability.

9 Slipstitch the center opening of the scarf.

1 Using the cut strips as described in the cutting instructions on p. 79, fold the long raw edges to the center and fold again. Twist the strip a few times and keep it twisted as you knot. (If your fabric for the knots is thin, you may want to "fill" it by putting another strip of fabric in the center of the fold of the first strip or inserting a small piece of rolled batting.)

2 Start an overhand knot in the middle of the strip, but don't pull the tail through; leave a loop.

3 Slip the free tail through the looped tail, and then tighten the loop by pulling the tail.

4 Make an opening between the strands in the knot with a nail, trim one tail, put a drop of glue in the opening, and tuck the tail into it. Repeat for the other tail.

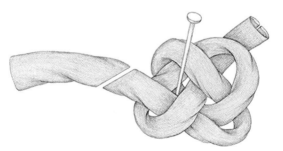

finished size
14¼ in. by 69 in.

artist
Stephanie Valley

materials
- 2 yd. China silk
- 2 yd. silk chiffon
- ⅛ yd. of 45-in.-wide
  metallic organza
- Bugle beads (various sizes
  and colors)
- Sequins (various sizes and colors)
- Glue stick
- Clear ruler
- Chalk marker
- Cotton or rayon thread
- Polyester thread
- Beading needle
- Hand-sewing needle
- Rotary cutter
- Cutting mat with grid
- Pattern weights
- Size 60 or 65 machine needle
- Walking foot
- Basic sewing kit (see pp. 4-8)

cutting instructions
Cut or tear two 15¼-in. by 70-in.
strips of China silk. One piece is
used as the lining.
Cut or tear one 15¼-in. by 70-in.
strip of silk chiffon.
Cut 92, 1¼-in. squares of metallic
organza.

beaded pockets

Two layers of China silk, a layer of silk chiffon,
some metallic organza squares, and a few beads create
a fanciful scarf with glittery pockets and quiltlike texture.
Iridescent, light as a feather, and ever-so-slightly secretive,
this scarf makes a wonderful evening accent
(or even a beautiful table runner).

1. With wrong side up, lay the short end of one piece of China silk on a cutting mat. Square up the fabric and align the raw edges with the grid lines. Keep in place with pattern weights.

2. Starting 1½ in. from each edge, evenly space seven metallic squares on top of the China silk, allowing ½ in. between each square (see the drawing below).

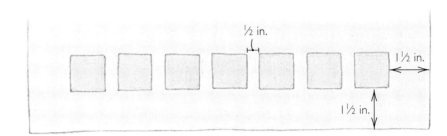

3. Lift each square one at a time to apply a small amount of glue. Reposition and allow to dry. Continue gluing five more rows of seven squares in an even grid. Use a clear ruler and a chalk marker, if necessary, for accurate alignment.

4. For the last (seventh) row, evenly space and glue four metallic squares, skipping three spaces, as shown in the drawing at right.

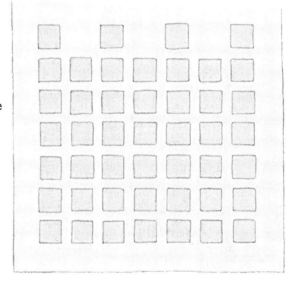

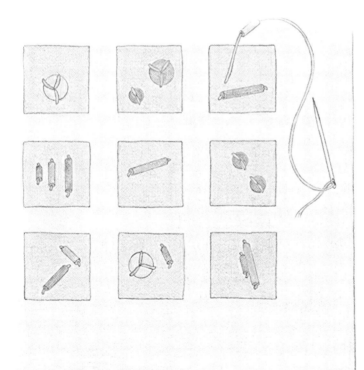

5. Using a beading needle and polyester thread, hand-sew bugle beads and/or sequins to each metallic square, sewing through both layers of fabric (see the drawing at left).

6. Repeat steps 1 through 5 at the other end of the China silk piece.

7 Pin the wrong side of the silk chiffon piece to the embellished side of the China silk. Pin frequently or hand-baste with silk thread in a large 6-in. grid pattern to anchor the two pieces together.

8 Using a chalk marker and a clear ruler, mark a parallel line ¼ in. from each last row of four squares. Using cotton or rayon thread and a 2.75mm stitch length, sew along the marked line through both layers.

9 Stitch seven more rows at both ends, each 1¾ in. apart and between rows of squares (see the drawing at right). Either mark each line of stitching with a chalk marker first or use the quilting guide arm on your sewing machine for even, parallel rows.

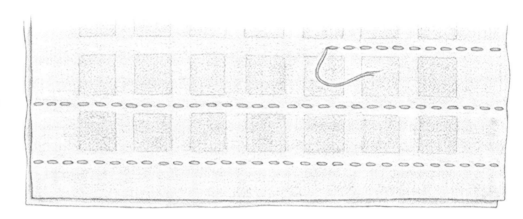

Using a walking foot (sometimes called an even-feed presser foot) will prevent the two layers of fabric from creeping and becoming distorted.

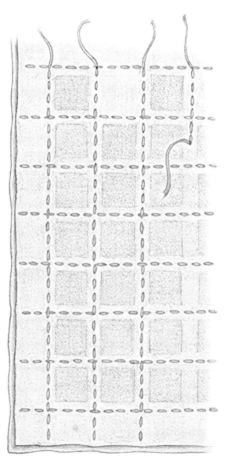

10 Using a chalk marker and clear ruler, mark lines perpendicular to the previously sewn rows, making 1¾-in. squares around each metallic square (see the drawing at right). Stitch all lines on both ends, creating small 1¾-in. square pockets. Tie off each thread tail to the underside where the stitching intersects with the last row.

11 Mark 23 parallel rows 1¾ in. apart through the center and unembellished portion of the scarf. Stitch through each line, as shown in the drawing below.

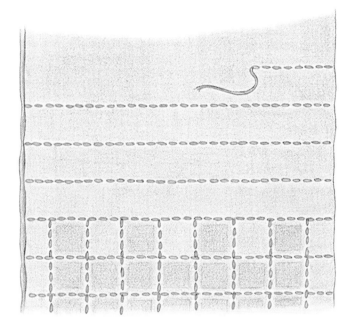

12 Trim the scarf edges evenly, leaving a 1-in. allowance from the outer rows of stitching. Trim to adjust the remaining piece of China silk to match the stitched and embellished piece.

13 With right sides together, pin the embellished scarf to the China silk. Stitch ½-in. seams on all edges, leaving an opening for turning. Trim the corners and gently press the seams open. Turn to the outside and slip-stitch the opening.

14 Using a beading needle and polyester thread, stitch one row of multicolored bugle beads end to end along each short end of the scarf (see the drawing below).

15 Determine the beading sequence for four beaded corners. Knot a length of thread (double if using polyester) and bring it through the hem at the scarf corner. Take a tiny stitch through all layers of fabric and add beads to the thread in the predetermined sequence. At the end of the bead sequence, pick up a seed bead and reroute the thread through the beads. Tie off, hiding the thread in the bugle beads.

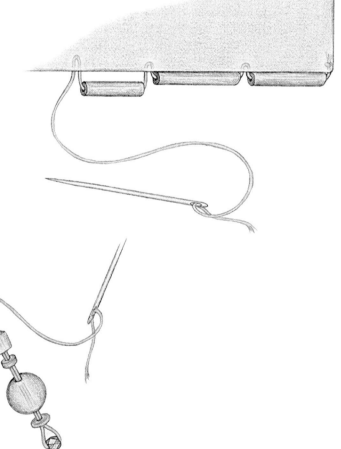

artist

Jane Conlon

materials

- 2 yd. rayon/silk cut velvet
- Seed beads, charlottes, or tri-cuts (one or many colors)
- Silk thread (any color)
- Nymo beading thread (lightest weight available)
- Beading needles (size appropriate for beads selected)
- Beeswax
- Hand-sewing needles
- Thread
- Basic sewing kit (see pp. 4-8))

fabric notes

Rayon/silk varieties of velvet are recommended for their draping qualities rather than cotton, which is too stiff. The velvet can be plain, crushed, or patterned, such as burn-out (dévoré).

If having the pattern on two sides is too busy because of the show-through, use chiffon, georgette, crepe de chine, charmeuse, or China silk for lining.

Three finished size variations are recommended: A 9-in. to 12-in. by 45-in. casual scarf requires ⅔ yd.; a 12-in. by 60-in. elegant scarf requires 1⅔ yd.; and a 20-in. to 24-in. by 72-in. opera scarf or shawl uses 2 yd.

cutting instructions

Cut two 25-in. by 73-in. pieces of cut velvet. One piece is used as the lining.

beaded fringe

Embellish a richly colored rayon/silk cut-velvet scarf with a beaded fringe that resembles netting. Vary the size for casual wear, elegant, or opera.

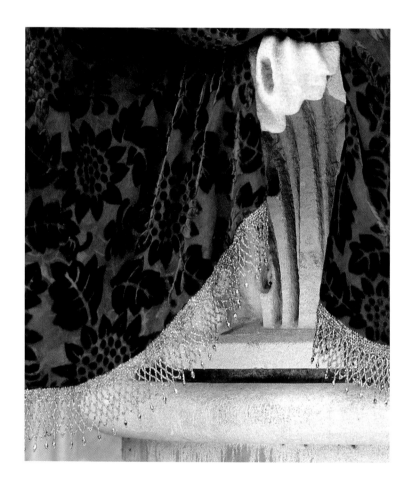

1 With right sides together, pin and baste the scarf and lining together. Refer to p. 15 for detailed instructions on sewing velvet. Stitch all sides, leaving an opening.

2 Trim and grade the seam allowances. Turn to the outside and slipstitch the opening. Press the scarf using the appropriate pressing aids for velvet (see p. 8).

To reduce the bulk of a seam, stitch the remaining seam allowance with a multi-zigzag stitch.

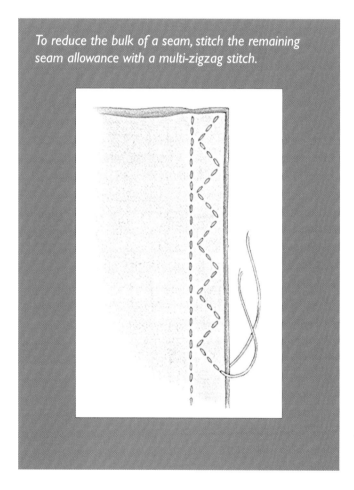

bead notes

Jane recommends using seed beads for the border and fringe, with contrasting beads, large beads, crystals, or pearls added at points where the open net intersects and at the bottom of the fringe. She especially likes size 13 charlotte beads, size 11 tri-cut beads, and size 13 Japanese delica beads. Select beads for their light-reflective properties.

To calculate the number of beads needed for your scarf, bead a 1-in. or 2-in. test sample, and then multiply the number of beads used by the width of the finished fringe. Buy extra beads.

The sample project uses 6½ hanks of size 11 tri-cut beads (12,000 beads), 1 hank of a matte bead for contrast (1300), and 80 crystals at the bottom of the fringe.

3 Understitch the lining using the prickstitch around the entire scarf (see p. 10). This helps keep the lining from falling away. The importance of understitching increases as the scarf gets larger.

4 Work the horizontal and vertical netted fringe across both ends of the scarf. The beaded fringe has two parts: from one to ten rows of a closely netted horizontal border and a loosely netted fringe of varying length and width.

   The horizontal netting is the more time-consuming part of the beaded fringe. At least one foundation row is recommended, but you can work as many rows as desired. Similarly, the length of the vertical fringe is variable.

   Work with slightly less than an arm's length of a single knotted strand of Nymo and try using it both waxed and unwaxed to see which way you prefer.

5 For the horizontal border, work from left to right with the end of the scarf away from you. Take a stitch in the fabric from back to front; secure with a backstitch. To begin the first row, pick up one bead only, take a stitch from back to front, and insert the needle through the bead. Subsequently, pick up two beads, take a stitch from back to front (a), then insert the needle through the last bead (b). Repeat to the end of the row.

a

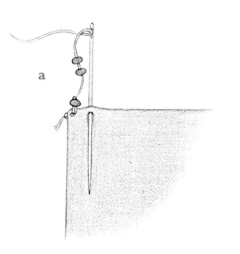

b

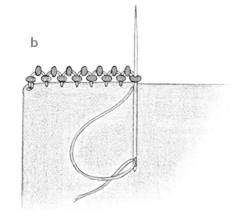

6 For additional rows, turn the scarf over and work the same way from left to right, sewing into the horizontal beads (as shown at right), then back through the last bead. Repeat for the desired number of rows, tying on new thread as needed.

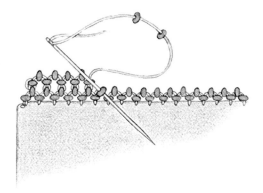

7 For the open fringe, work from left to right, with the end of the scarf toward you. Begin through the first bead in the last row of the border. Pick up the number of beads for the first sequence (five to eight work well), then a contrasting bead, then the next sequence. Repeat for the desired length of the fringe, using an odd number of sequences. At the end add dangles as shown, or create your own. Work back through the dangle, then repeat sequences, passing the needle through the contrasting beads of the first row as shown at right, to join the net.

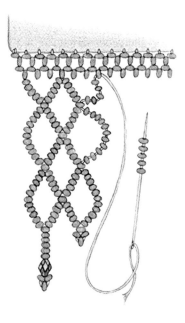

8 When back at the top, pass the needle through the third or fourth bead in the last row of the close border (or space as desired), and begin a new row of the fringe. Alternating the dangle design adds interest.

stenciled, stamped, and stitched

As artists, we cannot leave a plain piece of fabric alone.
Add a dab of paint with a brush, stamp, or stencil, stitch a few
designs inspired by a rooftop or an ethnic symbol, and an ordinary
fabric turns into a masterpiece. And it costs so little.

finished scarf

10⅝ in. by 76 in.

artist

Carol Spier

materials

- 1⅛ yd. silk shantung (scarf)
- 1⅛ yd. baby flannel (filler)
- Four colors of embroidery floss
- Hand embroidery needle
- Thread
- Clear ruler or template the width of the quilting grid
- Nonpermanent fabric marker
- Basic sewing kit (see pp. 4-8)

fabric notes

Wash the fabrics first to preshrink them.

Thai silk, silk douppioni, heavy China silk or wool challis, or something similarly soft but stable is suitable. The fabric should fringe interestingly.

thread notes

Pearl cotton, metallic thread, or novelty rayon thread may be substituted for the embroidery floss. Select an embroidery needle to accommodate the thread size you decide to use.

cutting instructions

SCARF

Cut one 21½-in. by 76-in. piece of silk.

FILLER

Cut one 10¼-in. by 72-in. piece of baby flannel.

simple
quilted silk

*This simple silk rectangle combines
the beautiful intricate stitching of classic sashiko
with the warmth and softness of a quilted blanket.
Make one to wear and one as a keepsake.*

1. To set up the quilting grid, divide the finished width of the scarf by five. Mark a sample grid on a scrap of the fabric, using the marker and ruler you'll use when you make the scarf. Measure the grid from side to side to be sure it equals the finished width of the scarf. If it doesn't, adjust one or the other. Success depends upon taking the time to set up the quilting grid accurately. If you don't plan the grid size realistically, it will end up off-center.

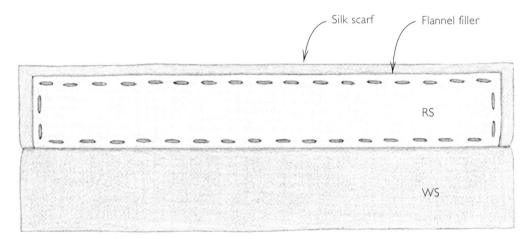

Silk scarf   Flannel filler

RS

WS

2. Press the scarf in half lengthwise, right side out. Open it out flat, wrong side up. Place the flannel on one half, centering it between the ends and between the fold and one seamline, as shown in the drawing at right. Baste the flannel to the scarf.

3. With right sides together, fold the scarf in half lengthwise. Sew the lengthwise seam. Press the seam open, trim if appropriate, turn the scarf right side out through one end, and press the seam and fold sharp.

4. Mark the lengthwise quilting lines on one side of the scarf. Using six strands of embroidery floss, quilt the marked line, making small neat stitches (see the drawing below and the sidebar on p. 96). Use four colors in regularly alternating sequence. Pin between the marked lines to hold the layers flat. Begin and end about 2 in. from each end.

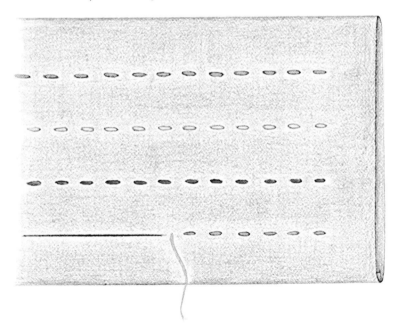

5 Mark and quilt the crosswise portion of the grid, centering the grid at the midpoint of the scarf's length.

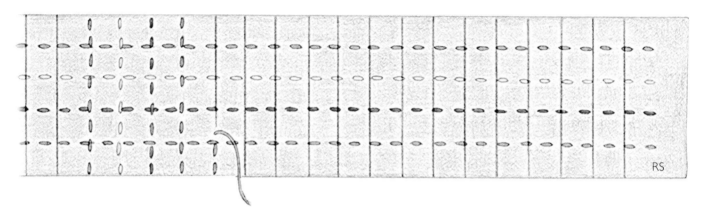

6 To fringe the ends of the scarf, carefully remove several crosswise threads. Remove any basting and the marked grid if anything remains of it. Press the scarf and enjoy it.

how to quilt

To begin the thread, insert the needle from the top and slide it between the layers at a slight diagonal, pointing it in the opposite direction from which you will be stitching. Bring it up on the marked line and pull it through, leaving a tail of thread where you inserted it. Turn and stitch. End in the same manner. When you are done, cut all the thread tails close to the fabric and lift the fabric to ease the remaining thread end between the layers.

Stand at a work table to quilt, with the scarf lying flat. Or if you are a stickler for uniform stitches, pin the scarf to some sort of frame for quilting.

stenciled and shaped

*Create your own fabric design using stencils
and fabric paint and work it into a pieced and edged scarf
with funky, pleated flaps on each end.*

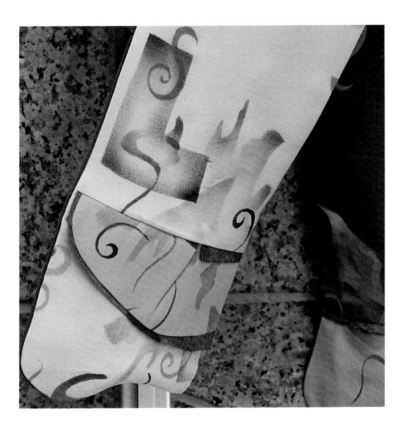

finished size

6 in. by 48 in.

artist

Diane Ericson

materials

- Two to four compatible fabrics
  (1 yd. total yardage)
- Thread
- Chalk marker
- Basic sewing kit (see pp. 4-8)
- Stenciling kit (see p. 100)

fabric notes

Choose flat-textured drapey rayon
or silk fabrics such as silk charmeuse,
silk crepe de chine, or sandwashed
rayon. A small amount of a print
fabric can be used as the flap lining
and as trims and edges.

cutting instructions

SCARF BODY (SIDE A)
Cut one piece of fabric 7½ in. wide
by 44 in. long. See step 1 on p. 98 for
details on cutting the ends.

SCARF END (SIDE A)
Cut one piece of the same fabric
7½ in. wide by 6½ in. long. See step 2
on p. 98 for details on cutting the ends.

SCARF BODY (SIDE B)
Cut one piece of fabric (different
from Side A) 6½ in. wide by 44 in.
long. See step 3 on p. 98 for details
on cutting the ends.

SCARF END (SIDE B)
Cut one piece of the same fabric
6½ in. wide by 6½ in. long. See step 4
on p. 98 for details on cutting the ends.

INSERT
Cut one 2½-in.-wide by 28-in.-long
piece of fabric.

FLAPS
Cut four 8-in.-wide by 5-in.-long
pieces of fabric. See step 5 on p. 98
for details on cutting the flaps to
shape.

TRIMS AND EDGES
Cut a few 2-in.-wide strips of fabric
in various lengths from 3 in. to 8 in.

1. Cut one end of the Side A scarf body at a right angle. Following the scaled pattern template 1 at right, cut the other end in a free-form soft curve.

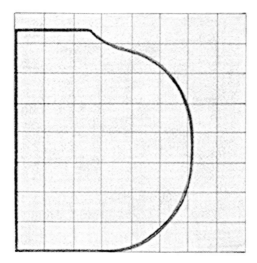

Template 1

1 square = 1 in.

2. Cut one end of the Side A scarf end at a right angle. Following the scaled pattern template 2 at right, cut the other end in a free-form soft curve.

Template 2

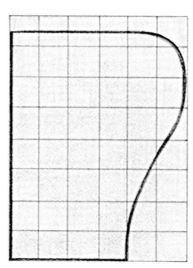

3. Cut one end of the Side B scarf body at a right angle. Following the scaled pattern template 2, cut the other end in a free-form soft curve.

4. Cut one end of the Side B scarf end at a right angle. Following the scaled pattern template 1, cut the other end in a free-form soft curve.

5. From the four flap rectangles, cut two flaps using pattern template 3 and the other two flaps using pattern template 4.

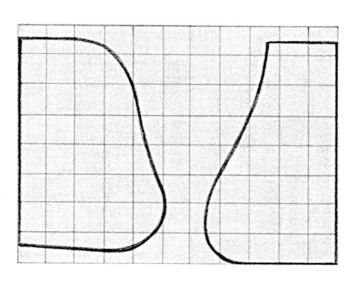

Template 3

Template 4

stenciling kit

- **Tracing paper**
- **Acetate for stencil material or precut stencil designs**
- **Small piece of glass, plastic mat, or layers of newspaper**
- **X-Acto knife**
- **Transparent tape**
- **Two or three pieces of dense foam sponge**
- **Small bowl for water**
- **Thick towel**
- **Fabric paints**
- **Plastic container lids or paper plates**
- **Sticks or spoons for mixing paints**
- **Paper towels**
- **Sponge brushes (optional)**

6 Stencil the designs on the fabric pieces.

7 To make Side A, begin with the right sides of two flaps together. Sew the flaps along the curved bottom and side only (a). Favor the lining side to the outside unevenly—as much as ½ in. at one end. With right sides together, sew the remaining straight side (b). Trim and clip the curves and turn to the outside. Press. Trim the top raw edges evenly to make about a 4½-in.-high flap.

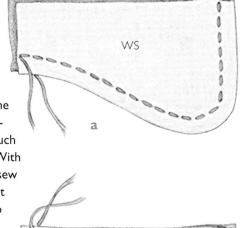

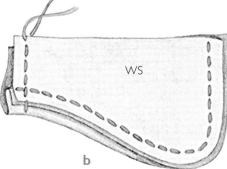

stenciling primer

There are a number of sources for precut stencils and designs, but creating and cutting your own designs is so simple that you really don't need to rely on precut ones. Look for inspiration from stencil books, stained-glass patterns, woodcuts, logos, symbols, and letter forms. Choose strong designs that are completely enclosed. Transfer the designs onto tracing paper.

On top of the tracing, tape a piece of acetate about 2 in. bigger all around than the design. Put the acetate/drawing layers on a cutting surface such as a strip of heavy glass, plastic mat, or layers of newspaper. Starting at the corners and cutting the smallest details first, cut out the designs with

an **X-Acto knife.** If you slip and cut beyond the design, simply cover the cut on both sides with transparent tape, rub it down, and recut the shape.

Spread your fabric materials out on a clean, covered surface. Rinse the foam sponge and then squeeze out as much water as you can. Wrap the sponge in a thick towel and squeeze it again. When the sponge has just a hint of moisture, it is ready to use.

Spoon a small amount of the paint colors onto the edge of lids or plates. Touch the sponge to the paint and dab it many times in a clean area until the paint impression looks even. Holding the edges

8 To make trims and edges, fold 2-in.-wide strips of fabric in half lengthwise with the wrong sides together and press. Cut a 4-in. strip. Fold the raw edges of one short end to the inside. Place the strip at one end and on the right side of the flap, matching the raw edges.

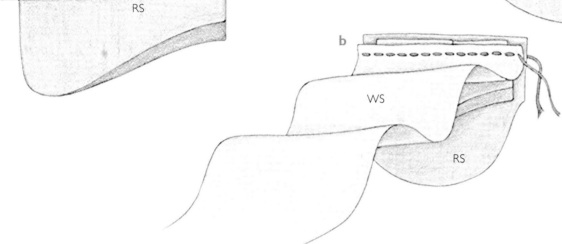

9 Center the wrong side of the flap on the right side of the Side A scarf end. Form a small ½-in. soft pleat in the upper edge of the flap, leaving seam allowances on both sides of the scarf (a). Matching all raw edges, position the Side A scarf body on top of the flap with the right sides together. Stitch a ½-in. seam (b). Press the seam toward the scarf body.

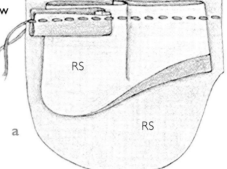

of the stencil gently on top of the fabric, pat through the stencil lightly but firmly. After you've printed over the entire design, lift off the stencil.

To print pastels, mix white directly into the color you'll use. If you want to print more vibrant light colors, you must do it in two stages. First, print the design with white paint in an even, thin coat. Allow the white to dry; then do a second application with the color on top. Experiment with layers of different colors, working all the colors wet. Then try allowing them to dry between layers. Try printing with more water for a hazy effect or dry-print over a dried-out watery layer. Experiment and play!

Once you've completed the printing and the paint is dry, heat-set the paint on the front and back with an iron and a press cloth. Use a heat setting recommended by the paint manufacturer and as hot as the fabric will handle. Heat setting will allow you to wash and dry the fabric.

Clean the acetate stencils after each use by placing them in a sink under warm running water. After a few minutes, gently rub the stencils with your fingers. Pat them dry between paper towels.

10 To make Side B, draw a 1½-in. by 27-in. rectangle in the center of the scarf body. Starting at one long edge, staystitch along the marked lines. Trim out the center of the rectangle, leaving ½-in. seam allowances and trimming to each corner, as shown in the drawing at right.

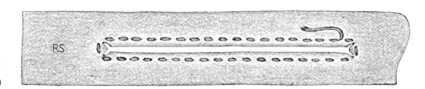

11 Fold the scarf body back along the staystitching line to expose one long seam allowance. Center one long raw edge of the insert along the seam allowance of the cutout with right sides together. Sewing on the scarf body side and using the stay-stitching as a guide, stitch a ½-in. seam. Fold the adjacent edges back and stitch each side of the rectangle separately. Press the seam allowances toward the scarf body.

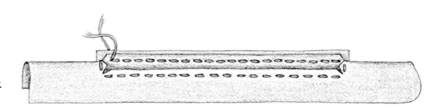

12 Construct the flap and trim for Side B as in steps 7 and 8.

13 Attach the trimmed flap to the scarf end and body as in step 9.

14 Referring to step 8, make one 8-in.-long trim piece. With right sides together and matching edges, position the trim on one long side and toward the end of Side B. Baste in place (see the drawing below).

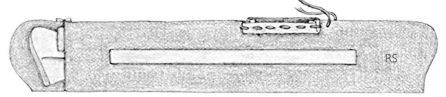

15 Aligning the raw edges, pin Side A to Side B with the right sides together. The flaps will be at opposite ends. Stitch around all edges, leaving a 4-in. opening. Trim the seams at the curves and turn to the outside. Slip-stitch the opening.

16 Press the scarf in half, creating a new edge with about ½ in. of Side A showing on Side B (see the drawing below).

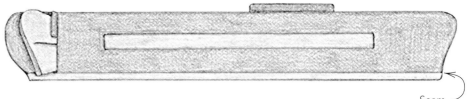

Seam

remnant queen's ribbons

Cut strips of the softest of silks to make ribbon strips, stamp and embellish to create unique designs, and piece to perfection to make this one-of-a-kind scarf.

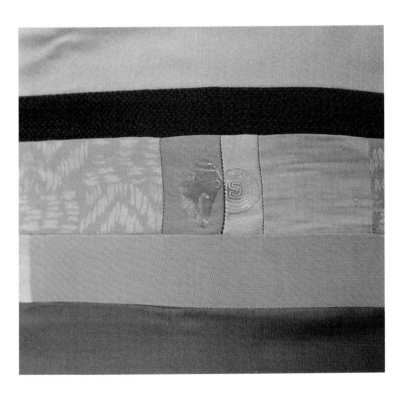

finished size

10½ in. by 64 in.

artist

Marcy Tilton

materials

- ⅛-yd. to ¼-yd. pieces of 7 to 10 remnants (scarf body)
- ⅜ yd. soft crinkled metallic gauze (bottom edge)
- Thread
- Fabric paints
- Plastic painter's palette
- Rubber stamps
- Sponge paintbrush or finely textured sponges
- Basic sewing kit (see pp. 4-8)

fabric notes

Assemble a group of fabric scraps of fluid, natural-fiber fabrics like silk crepe de chine, rayon crepe, silk jacquard, 4-ply silk, or hand-painted silk for the scarf body. Two-sided fabrics like crepe-back charmeuse and jacquards add to the interest of the mix.

cutting instructions

SCARF BODY

Tear or pull threads and cut a batch of strips of uneven widths along the crosswise grain. The width of the fabric determines the length of the body of the scarf. The combination of widths should add up to 21 in.

INSERTS

Tear or cut extra strips for stamping

END

Tear or cut two 8-in. by 21-in. strips of metallic gauze.

1 Lay out the fabric strips on a flat surface to see which colors to combine. Design each lengthwise strip one at a time, making sure to stagger the seams of the piecing.

2 Stamp a variety of fabric widths and colors to use as small inserts or use scraps of hand-painted silk or interesting patterned fabric.

3 With right sides together, assemble each lengthwise strip first, stitching ¼-in. seams and pressing open. Then stitch each lengthwise strip together to make the width of the scarf (21 in. finished). True the ends by pulling a thread in each pieced section and trimming evenly.

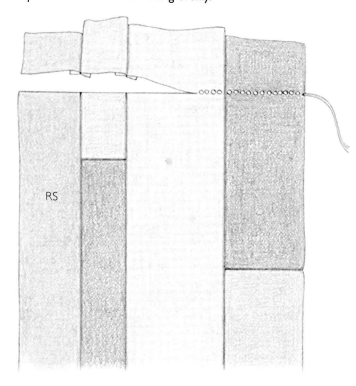

all about stamping

Marcy uses a combination of purchased and hand-carved rubber stamps—some made for paper, others for fabric. Choose images with related and harmonious shapes and designs. Sometimes a fragment of the stamp is more pleasing than the whole image. Experiment on scraps to be sure you like the impression on fabric.

Mix the fabric paints in a plastic painter's palette. Using a sponge paintbrush or finely textured sponges, apply the paint with a dabbing motion and experiment with the amount of paint that gives the result you want. Keep cleaning the stamp to prevent buildup and blurring.

The first batch of experimental stamped images can be used for small inserts. Look for interest and character, random effects and variety.

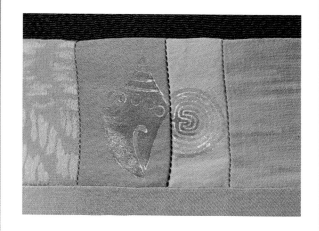

4 Inserts should be on the straight of grain and wider than the width of the lengthwise strip. With right sides together, place the insert to the end of a lengthwise strip, matching the short edge of the insert to one raw edge of the lengthwise strip. Sew a 1/4-in. to 3/8-in. seam. Press the seam flat. Trim the insert to the exact width of the lengthwise strip by pulling a thread and cutting along the thread line. Press the seam open or to one side, depending on the "lay" of the fabric.

> When joining one strip to another, do not use pins. Align the edges carefully and stitch as straight and true as possible. Using pins causes thin fabric to get wavy. If you want to hold each seam in place, baste with silk thread first.

Offset seam allowances.

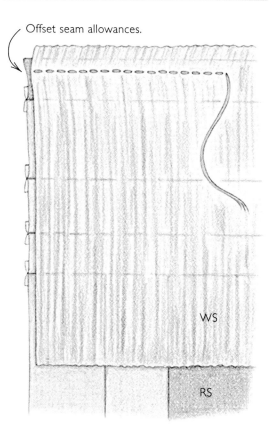

WS

RS

5 Sew several stamped strips together horizontally to make two 5-in. by 21-in. sections. With right sides together, sew one horizontal section to each end of the scarf body, as shown in the drawing below.

6 With right sides together, stitch the long edge of the metallic gauze band to each end of the scarf (see the drawing at left). Because metallic gauze is loosely woven, a narrow seam could easily pull out. To prevent this, offset the seam allowances by stitching a 1/4-in. seam on the silk scarf and a 1/2-in. seam on the gauze.

7 Fold the scarf in half lengthwise with the right sides together. Stitch the long edge. Press the seam open and turn the scarf to the right side.

8 Turn each gauze end to the inside, folding in half to cover the seam allowance. Stitch in the ditch or slipstitch to the underside.

home away
from home

Inspired by house architectural details,
this whimsical scarf is not only fascinating for its unique
design but also for the use of ribbons as prairie-point
rooftops and for the fun, decorative stitching.

finished size
10 in. by 60 in.

artist
Marcy Tilton

materials
- 1⅔ yd. each of two colors of soft fluid fabric
- ½-yd. lengths of 12 to 18 different soft ribbons in an assortment of widths
- Two spools of rayon variegated decorative thread, size 48
- Thread
- Hand sewing needle
- Tagboard
- Gridded cutting mat
- Clo-chalk removable tailor's chalk
- Basic sewing kit (see pp. 4-8)

fabric notes
Select fluid fabrics such as rayon Tencel, rayon jacquards, sandwashed rayon or silk, rayon or wool challis, or lightweight wool jersey for the scarf. Certain fabrics, such as rayon Tencel, have an interesting selvage that can be featured on the long edges of the scarf. Find beautiful ribbons such as rayon grosgrain, vintage satin, hand-painted silk bias ribbon, and organza. Choose an assortment of widths ranging from ⅜ in. to 2 in.

cutting instructions
Cut 10¾-in. by 60-in. fabric rectangles. Use two different colors or the same. Press flat, trimming loose threads.

See details on p. 108 for preparing the ribbon lengths.

construction

1 When using the selvage for one edge, press the raw edge under only. To ensure pressing accuracy, make a tagboard template 2 in. wide by 15 in. long. Draw a line on the tagboard ⅜ in. from one long edge. Place the template about ⅜ in. from the raw edge and press the fabric up and over the template even with the drawn line. Press through the fabric and template. If you don't plan to use the selvage, don't press the edges under.

2 Make approximately 75 prairie-point roof tops out of 12 to 18 different ribbons (see the sidebar below).

---

how to make prairie points

Working with ½-yd. lengths of various ribbons, hold one end of the ribbon with one hand. With the other hand, fold the opposite end down and at a right angle, creating a diagonal fold (a). Finger-press or press with an iron. Fold the right-angled end down, aligning inside ribbon edges and creating a sharp point at the top (b). Press.

a

b

The exposed lengths of the finished points can range from ½ in. to 2¼ in. Depending on the lengths of each point, the ½ yd. of ribbon will yield several prairie points.

Consider embellishing the ribbon first or altering the material in some way before making the points. Embellish 2-in. double satin ribbon by pressing it in half lengthwise and stitching ¼ in. from the woven edge using rayon decorative thread in a serpentine stitch (see the drawing at right).

RS

If a ribbon such as hand-painted silk bias is too flimsy to use as one layer, make a tube by stitching lengthwise in a narrow seam, turning inside out, and pressing (see the drawing below). The seam makes an interesting detail.

WS   RS

---

3 Working on a gridded cutting mat, place the cut ends of the ribbon prairie points on the right side of one rectangle and even with the edges of the scarf. Cluster the points at each end to look like a city skyline (see the drawing below). Experiment with various sizes and lengths to see which colors and shapes look best together. Play with the relationship of size, color, and texture. Check the effect from both sides. Add a few extra points to fill in the gaps as needed. Hand-baste in place using rayon thread.

4 With right sides together, place the plain scarf piece on the section trimmed with prairie points. Stitch the short ends together with a ½-in. seam (see the drawing below). Turn and press. If you are not using the selvage as a decorative edge, continue to sew the long edges also, leaving an opening. Turn to the outside and slip-stitch the opening.

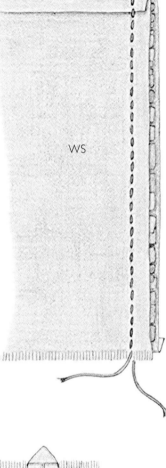

WS

RS

5 Working on a pressing surface, press the long folded edge into place, butting the fold to the woven portion of the selvage "fringe." Hand-baste with rayon thread. Insert small prairie-point rooftops in a random pattern to represent the suburbs or country (see the drawing at right). Baste a 6-in. to 8-in. section at a time. Continue to place points and hand-stitch on both long sides. Using thread that matches each side, topstitch the edges through all layers.

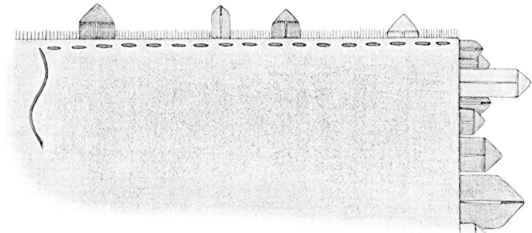

6 Machine-stitch your house design on the scarf. Sketch the design on paper before you draw it on fabric and make a sample before you begin. Use Clo-chalk removable tailor's chalk to draw the design on the fabric. Since the chalk will fade while working on the scarf, draw a portion of the overall design only, stitch that portion, and draw more.

Starting in the center and working toward the ends, stitch over the design using rayon variegated decorative thread and a 2.5mm stitch length. Do as much continuous drawing/stitching as possible to minimize thread tails. The thread is so soft that you can stitch over a line several times without it getting too stiff, and the additional lines and designs add definition and depth. Stitch the house shapes first, and then go back and add windows.

Begin stitching with one stitch forward and one stitch backward. This is enough to keep the slippery thread from pulling out as you work, but it is not permanent. If you back-stitch and clip the thread, it will fray, get fuzzy, and look messy. Therefore, leave a long thread tail to tie off between layers with a quilter's knot (see below). Tie off threads in sections as you work to keep from stitching over them.

quilter's knot

Thread the tails into a hand sewing needle and make a knot in the thread close to the fabric. Insert the needle at the place where the thread emerges, sliding it between the two layers of cloth to bury the knot. Pull the needle out and clip the thread.

For design inspiration, collect house images from magazines, postcards, and books. A wonderful source is South of France, A Sketchbook by Sara Midda, published by Workman Publishing, New York (1990). Practice drawing, doodling, and sketching before you begin.

silk-screened velvet

This scarf project introduces you to the world of dyeing and making a silk-screen image using a thermal fax machine. Hand-crushed velvet, silk-screened with Mexican-inspired scroll symbols and lined with contrasting hand-dyed silk georgette, is the ultimate in luxury yet completely wearable for any occasion.

finished size
24 in. by 72 in.

artist
Holly Badgley

materials
- 2 yd. white rayon/silk velvet
- 2 yd. white silk double georgette
- Thread
- Access to a thermal fax machine (see Resources on p. 152)
- Thermal screen mesh
- Plastic frame for thermal screen
- Mounting tape
- Basic sewing kit (see pp. 4-8)
- Dyeing kit (see p. 112 and Resources on p. 152)

fabric notes

In order for the velvet fabric to dye well, it must be a rayon pile on a silk backing or 100% silk—no synthetics. Use silk double georgette rather than polyester or other blends. If you choose not to dye the velvet and double georgette fabrics with Procion MX dyes, buy the fabrics in beautiful contrasting colors of your choice or dye them in premixed liquid dyes that are readily available in grocery stores and craft outlets.

cutting instructions

SCARF
Cut one 25-in. by 73-in. piece of rayon/silk velvet.

LINING
Cut one 25-in. by 73-in. piece of silk double georgette.

1. Dissolve ¼ cup soda ash and ¼ cup Synthrapol detergent in water in a washing machine. Wash and dry the scarf fabric and lining to scour and preshrink.

---

dyeing kit

- **Soda ash**
- **Synthrapol detergent**
- **Urea**
- **Sodium alginate**
- **Three colors of Procion MX dyes**
- **Baking soda**
- **Water**
- **Blender**
- **Measuring spoons and cups**
- **Mask**
- **Rubber gloves**
- **Hard, porous surface such as a scrap of laminate countertop**
- **Foam brush, old credit card, or squeegee**

---

4. The thickened dye needs to be activated right before you use it. Mix four parts baking soda to one part soda ash. Dissolve these in just enough water to make a smooth paste. Add 1 tsp. of paste to one cup of thickened dye and stir well. Add only to the dye you will be using that day. This activated mixture will last only about five hours and then it will be unusable.

2. To prepare a chemical medium, dissolve 10 tbsp. of urea in 4 cups of warm water in a blender. With the blender still agitating gently, add 1 tbsp. sodium alginate, which is a thickener that becomes gelatinous after mixing. Let the blender run a bit more to decant the mixture and let it settle at least four hours before using.

3. Wearing a mask and rubber gloves, mix each powdered dye color in a small amount of water to dissolve it. This is called a slurry. To make thickened dye, mix each slurry with the chemical medium. (See the chart below for the formula.)

   The amount of slurry that is added to the chemical medium may vary, depending on the brand of dye, the kind of fabric selected, and the intensity of color you desire. For a medium shade, start with ½ tsp. slurry per one cup of chemical medium and adjust from there. You will need to experiment with quantities to obtain the saturation that you prefer.

   Record the formula that you are using—write everything down that goes into your color. The thickened dye will last for about a month.

Using the following formula, mix the slurry in the chemical medium to make thickened dye:

To 1 cup* of chemical medium add the following amounts of slurry:

- **To dye the velvet: ¾ tsp. dusty rose**
- **To dye the georgette: 2 tsp. chartreuse, ½ tsp. burnt orange**
- **To silk-screen a black image on velvet: 2 tbsp. black**
- ***At least 2 cups of each color of thickened dye are needed to paint each side of the scarf.**

5 Select a single image or motif and make a good, dense photocopy on white paper (see the drawings below).

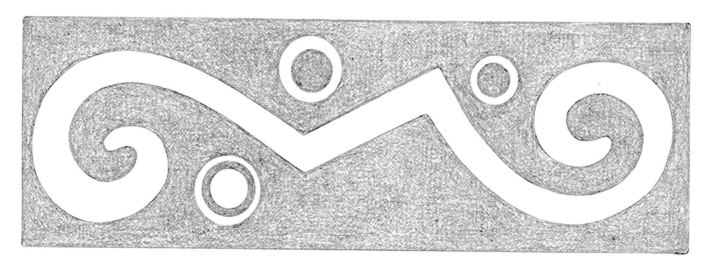

6 Place the photocopied image in the thermal fax machine. Run the thermal screen mesh through the machine following the manufacturer's instructions. The screen is light sensitive. The thermal fax machine's toner removes part of the silk-screen material, leaving a semisheer negative space as the image.

> ### *thermal fax machines*
>
> **Thermal fax machines are available as reconditioned units for a fraction of the original price. If you wish to experiment with the process before committing to purchase a machine, call your local office-products dealer and ask to rent or simply use a machine on their premises. The thermal screens, plastic frames, and mounting tape are purchased separately. (See Resources on p. 152.)**

7 Using the mounting tape, secure the screen to the plastic frame. This makes a rigid silk-screen usable for printing.

8 Position the velvet fabric, with the pile side up, on a hard, porous surface such as a scrap of plastic-laminate countertop. Place the silk-screen on top of the velvet. Using a foam brush, an old credit card, or a small squeegee, apply the thickened dye over the mesh. You'll need to test how much dye to apply (especially on velvet) to get a clean and even image. Allow the dye to dry thoroughly.

Plastic frame

Screen

9 Using the Synthrapol detergent, wash the velvet and georgette fabrics. To avoid color bleeding, wash each fabric separately. Dry both fabrics in a conventional dryer, but remove the velvet while it's still damp. Squeeze, twist, and texturize the fabric. The wetter the fabric, the more crushed the results. Crushing the fabric not only gives the fabric a more interesting look and light reflectance but also ensures that the fabric does not have to be handled so carefully when wearing.

Sewing velvet to another fabric that has a smooth surface can be very tricky. If a hand-basted running stitch doesn't keep the two fabrics from creeping, hand-sew a diagonal basting stitch (see p. 9).

10 With right sides together, pin the scarf and lining pieces together. Hand-baste with a small running stitch around all four edges. Machine-stitch, leaving an opening. Trim the seams and corners and turn to the outside. Slipstitch the opening.

finished size

14 in. by 60 in.

artist

Holly Badgley

materials

- 1¾ yd. white or off-white
  silk noil (raw silk)
- Thread
- Tagboard
- Basic sewing kit (see pp. 4-8)
- Dyeing kit (see p. 118 and
  Resources on p. 152)

fabric notes

Select natural-fiber fabrics such as silk noil and other raw silks, rayon/silk velvet, linen, and lightweight wool. The instructions and formulas given here are based on using Procion MX dyes, but other brands will work.

cutting instructions

Cut one 18-in. by 64-in. piece of silk noil. These dimensions allow for shrinkage when washed. The scarf will be cut to size later.

painted silk

*Using thickened dye as a painting medium,
cover whole areas of natural-fiber fabrics with interesting
motifs inspired by ancient symbols, nature's forms, or other
interesting shapes and patterns.*

1. Dissolve ¼ cup soda ash and ¼ cup Synthrapol detergent in water in a washing machine. Wash and dry the scarf fabric to scour and preshrink.

dyeing kit

- **Soda ash**
- **Synthrapol detergent**
- **Urea**
- **Sodium alginate**
- **Procion MX dyes (see instructions for colors used in this scarf project)**
- **Baking soda**
- **Water**
- **Blender**
- **Measuring spoons and cups**
- **Pencil or fabric marker**
- **Mask**
- **Rubber gloves**
- **Hard, porous surface such as a scrap of laminate countertop**
- **Three sizes of foam brushes**

5. To make a thickened dye, mix each slurry with the chemical medium. (See the chart at right for the formula and refer to step 3 for the Silk-screened Velvet scarf on p. 112 for detailed instructions.)

   Record the formula that you are using—write everything down that goes into your color. The thickened dye will last for about a month.

2. Using resources such as art books and magazines, old fabric designs, postcards, and other graphic materials, sketch an overall design to scale on paper. For a beginning project, limit the number of design motifs, sections, and colors.

3. Transfer the design to the scarf fabric. Designs can be transferred by using combinations of methods. Draw a design directly on the fabric using a pencil or fabric marker. Cut tagboard templates of the shapes and draw around them. Templates are especially useful around curves. Or cut through a full-scale design template with an X-Acto knife at the corners of the different sections, marking these significant points with a pencil and connecting the dots on the fabric.

4. To prepare a chemical medium, follow the directions given in step 2 for the Silk-screened Velvet scarf (see p. 112).

The saturation formula for the color palette (Holly has named it the ZaZu palette) in this scarf project is as follows:

To 1 cup* of chemical medium add the following amounts of slurry:

- **Pewter (background):** 1½ tsp. pewter
- **Grass:** 2 tsp. chartreuse, 1 tsp. avocado
- **Gold:** 1½ tsp. marigold, ½ tsp. burnt orange, ⅛ tsp. desert
- **Periwinkle:** ½ tsp. midnight, 1/16 tsp. desert
- **Teal (silk screen):** 1 tsp. teal blue

*One cup of thickened dye is adequate for most design elements on a scarf. Depending on your design, the background may require more dye (about 2 cups).

6 To activate the thickened dye before you use it, follow the directions given in step 4 for the Silk-screened Velvet scarf (see p. 112).

7 With the right side up, lay the fabric on a slightly textured but hard, porous surface such as a scrap piece of laminate countertop. Varying the size and width of foam brushes, paint each design section with the activated thickened dye.

8 Silk-screen designs can be added at this time. See the Silk-screened Velvet scarf project for silk-screening instructions (pp. 114-115).

9 Allow the fabric to set overnight and to dry slowly. If the fabric dries too quickly, the colors will not take.

10 Using the Synthrapol detergent, which releases the dye residue, wash the scarf fabric in a washing machine. You may want to wash it first in a utility sink before using a good washing machine. Dry in a dryer.

11 Press the fabric. Re-cut the fabric to 16 in. by 62 in.

12 Referring to p. 8 (pressing hems using tagboard templates), press finished 1-in. hems to the wrong side, as shown in the drawing at right. Miter the corners (see p. 15). Baste along the inside folded edges. Topstitch 7/8 in. from all edges.

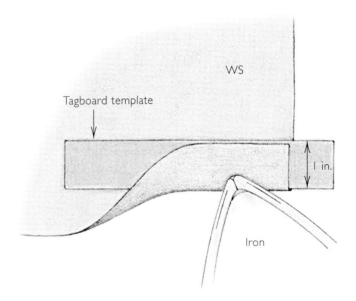

WS

Tagboard template

1 in.

Iron

architectural
shapes

When common shapes such as the rectangle
intersect, fold, gather, and button, an amazing thing happens.
A scarf is born that is engineered to function, to change,
and to bedazzle. Some are puzzles, some have variations,
all are truly fun to make and to wear.

buttons
and buttonholes

*Two reversible scarves can be worn solo or attached
with clever knotted buttons and buttonholes and worn as a
pair. Mixed prints and fabrics add an element of mystery
to just how many fabrics there really are.*

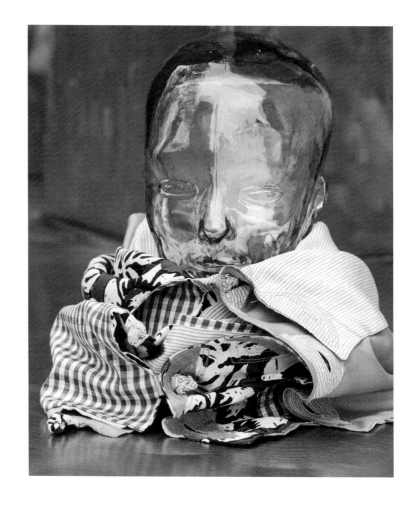

1 Fold each piping strip in half lengthwise with the wrong sides together. Press.

2 On the right side of a scarf piece and matching raw edges, pin the strips to the long edges. Starting a few inches from one end, use one strip along one edge and two strips along the other edge of each scarf piece (see the drawing at right). Overlap the two strips so that one will project more from the edge than the other and expose both strips from one side when finished. There's no formula for the placement of the strips. Use your intuition to choose the fabric combinations and place at random. Repeat this process to complete two trimmed scarf pieces.

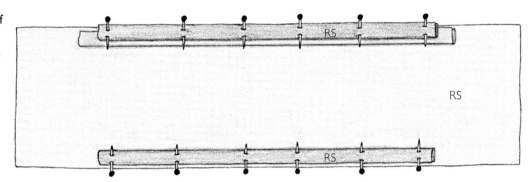

3 To finish the ends of the strips, fold the ends diagonally and match the raw edges.

4 Baste all strips to the scarf pieces.

5 Using the 8½-in.-long strips of fabric, make eight knotted buttons. With wrong sides together, fold each strip in half lengthwise. Press. Fold each raw edge to the center crease. The folded strips can be pressed or left as soft edges.

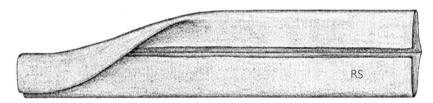

6 Tie a loose knot in the center of the strip. To beef up the knot, pull one end of the strip through the knot again.

7 Tie one more knot onto the first knot.

8 On the right side of each trimmed scarf piece and matching the raw edges, evenly space four knots across one short end. The first knot should begin about 1½ in. from one end. Baste both raw ends of the knotted buttons down (see the drawing below).

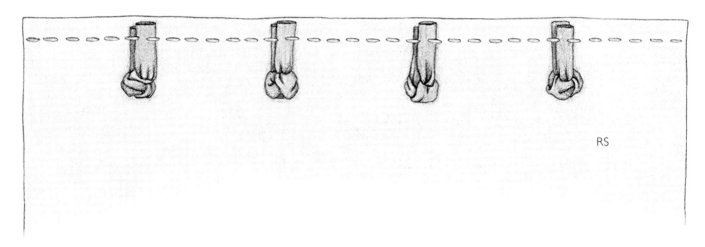

RS

9 With right sides together, pin the corresponding scarf pieces to the trimmed pieces. Sew all four sides of each scarf, leaving an opening. Trim the corners and turn the scarf to the outside. Slipstitch the opening. Press.

For accurate seam allowances, keep the trimmed side of the scarf up and sew along the previously sewn basting lines.

10 To make the buttonholes, first mark the placement of four buttonholes on each scarf to correspond with the knotted buttons on the opposite end. Aligning the longest raw edge of each triangle with the finished scarf edge, pin the right side of four raw-edged triangles to either side of the plain end of each scarf. Select your fabrics carefully. These triangles are visible on one side of the scarf.

⓫ Stitching through all layers, sew an almond-shaped circle large enough for the knotted button to slip through (see the drawing below). Make a test sample for size on a scrap of fabric. Clip through the center of the oval and to the ends of the almond shape. Pull the triangle through the opening to the opposite side of the scarf. Press.

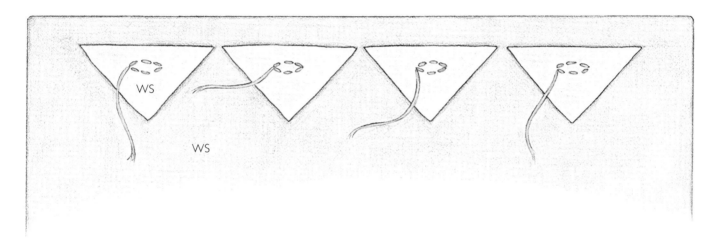

⓬ Starting with a line of stitching parallel to the opening, sew a concentric spiral around the opening until all of the triangle is sewn down (see the drawing at right). Have fun with the thread colors. Use matching or contrasting thread with one color on top and another in the bobbin. Press.

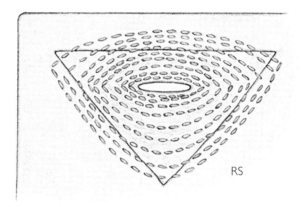

For an interesting variation, use shapes other than triangles for the buttonholes, such as squares, circles, diamonds, or stars. Sew two triangles on one side and two on the other, using different fabrics for each opening.

Wear an individual scarf loosely draped around your neck and hanging free. Or button the two scarves together and casually wrap once or twice. Button just a few of the knots or all of them. Change the fabrics that show to customize your ensemble.

finished size
9 in. by 54 in.

artist
Susan B. Allen

materials

- ¼ yd. vintage kimono fabric (center motif)
- 1 yd. corded silk (framing fabric)
- 1½ yd. textured silk charmeuse (lining)
- Thread
- Four buttons
- 5-in. by 20-in. clear, gridded quilter's ruler
- Erasable fabric marking pen
- Basic sewing kit (see pp. 4-8)

fabric notes

See the sidebar on p. 128 for notes on the fabric for the center motif, framing fabric, and lining.

cutting instructions

CENTER MOTIF
Cut six 4-in. squares.

FRAMING PIECES
Cut (or tear) five 4-in.-wide strips on the lengthwise grain. Do not piece. If you want to conserve fabric or feature a particular texture or pattern, the fabric may be cut on the crossgrain.

LINING
Do *not* cut the lining fabric until all squares are sewn together. At that time, take an accurate final measurement and cut the lining the same size as the finished scarf front.

pieced squares

*Using an easy piecing technique
(inspired by the timeless "Log Cabin" quilt pattern),
sew handsome fabrics into 9-in. squares, then join the
squares into a scarf. Leave an opening at each end to wear
the scarf looped through itself. Use interesting buttons
to affix end sections to the scarf body.*

fabric notes

center-motif fabric

Choose an elegant fabric such as a vintage kimono, a hand-dyed shibori or batik, damask, tapestry, or organza. This fabric can be slightly stiff because it's used in such small pieces that it shouldn't make the scarf unbending.

framing fabric

This fabric is sewn on all sides, surrounding the center. It should be rich and very drapey, like a corded silk, lightweight crepe, or soft chenille, velvet, or gabardine twill. A slight weave pattern adds a directional contrast when the pieces are sewn together. For the best look, the color of the framing fabric should contrast with the center.

lining fabric

Use a fluid silk crepe de chine or plissé. Don't use a typical lining fabric of polyester or rayon. The framing fabric can also be used as the lining selection.

The secret to this beautiful scarf is to use a gridded ruler to keep the pieces parallel and perpendicular and a fade-away marking pen to mark the lines before you sew.

1 With right side up, place a 4-in. square of center fabric on a flat surface. Refer to the grainline chart below for information on lining the fabric pieces up in the right direction. With right sides together and matching two raw edges, lay a strip of framing fabric over the center fabric and pin (see the bottom drawing). To make sure each seam is perfectly straight, use a clear gridded ruler to line up all sections and draw a straight seamline with a fabric marker. Stitch. Trim the seam to ¼ in.

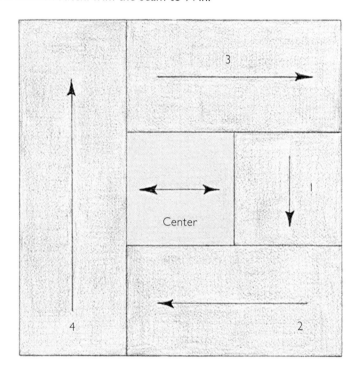

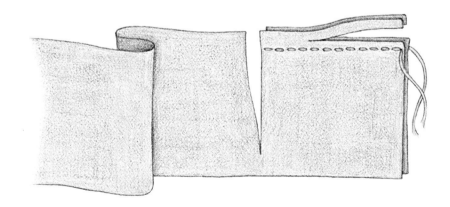

2 Trim the excess. The remaining portion of the strip will be used in the next step. From the wrong side, press the seam allowance toward the framing fabric. Press again on the right side of the fabric, using a press cloth to avoid permanent press marks.

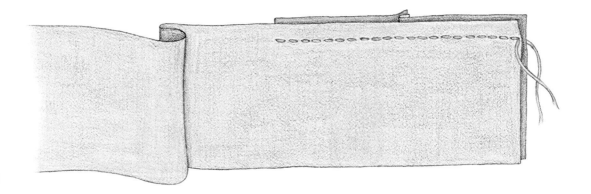

3 With right sides together and matching two raw edges, lay the framing strip along one long edge of the pieced section. Stitch the seam, trim the excess strip, and press toward the framing fabric. Continue to use the clear gridded ruler and marking method as described in step 1 for all of the piecing; otherwise, things will get out of square before you realize it.

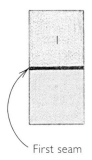

First seam

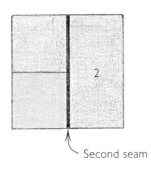

Second seam

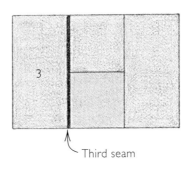

Third seam

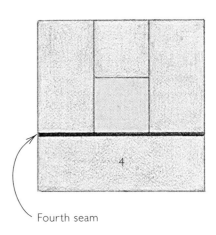

Fourth seam

4 Following the pattern as illustrated, continue to piece the framing strips to the center motif. Use the same marking, trimming, and pressing suggestions. Make a total of six squares. (To lengthen the scarf, add one or more squares. Do not enlarge the squares themselves.)

5 With right sides together, align the long edge of one square with the pieced edge of another square (see the drawing below). Matching raw edges, stitch a ½-in. seam. Continue in this pattern and sew four squares together.

6 Measure the length and width of the four-square strip (about 10 in. by 37 in.) and cut a piece of lining to match. Cut lining to match the two remaining squares, which should be about 10 in. by 10 in.

7 With right sides together, place the backing fabrics over the sections and pin. Lightly stretch the backing fabric to encourage it to curl under just a bit in the finished scarf. Stitch four sides, leaving an opening 4 in. to 5 in. long for turning. Trim the seams, turn to the outside, and slipstitch the opening. Press.

8 With the pieced sides up, place one edge of the individual squares 1 in. under each end of the four-piece section. Sew the buttons through both scarf layers near the long edges.

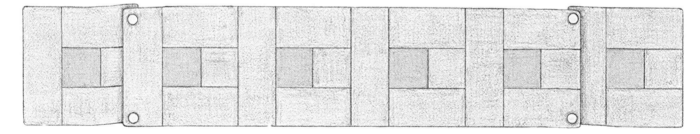

Put your hands through the openings and wear this scarf as a shawl. Or simply drape around your neck. Or thread one end through the opening at the opposite end.

self-connecting squares

*This scarf features a finished opening
at each end, allowing the wearer to slide one end through
the other, creating an overlapping angular effect to fill
a jacket or blouse neckline.*

finished size

6 in. by 46 in.

artist

Susan B. Allen

materials

- ¾ yd. silk (primary fabric)
- ¼ yd. each of two silk coordinates (accents)
- Four small buttons or beads
- Thread
- Basic sewing kit (see pp. 4-8)

fabric notes

The primary silk used in the original project is washed silk charmeuse. The accent fabrics are two colors of silk jacquard. Soft drapey fabrics such as crepe de chine and rayon may also be used. The inserts are interesting in a stripe fabric.

cutting instructions

PRIMARY FABRIC

Cut two 29-in. by 7-in. pieces (scarf body and lining).
Cut two 7-in. by 7-in. pieces (ends).

ACCENTS

From one of the ¼-yd. pieces, cut four 6½-in. by 7-in. pieces (inserts).
From the other ¼-yd. piece, cut four 1½-in. by 7-in. pieces (insert trims).

1 With right sides together, stitch one long edge of an insert trim strip to the 7-in. side of an insert (a). To complete a tubular section, sew the other long edge of the insert trim to the other 7-in. side (b). Trim and press the seams toward the accent piece. Repeat for the remaining three accent sections.

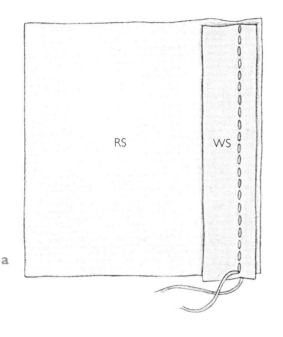

RS

WS

a

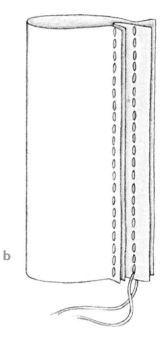

b

2 With wrong sides together, press the tubes in half lengthwise to form ¼-in.-wide weltlike trim on one side of each accent section.

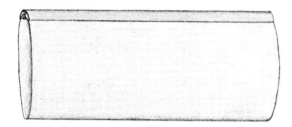

3 Position two accent sections on the right side of the end of each end piece. Butt the ¼-in. trims at the center, leaving ½ in. on each side of the end piece. Stitch. Trim the seam and press toward the end piece.

4 Fold under the opposite ½-in. seam allowance of each end piece and press.

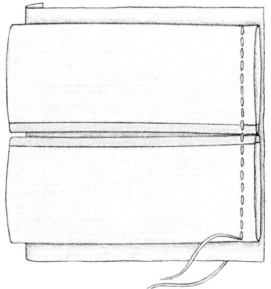

5 With right sides together, fold the end piece in half cross-wise. Stitch each side seam, making sure not to catch the accent sections (see the drawing below).

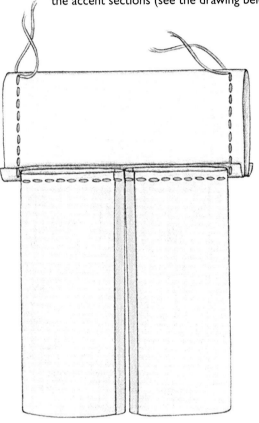

6 Trim the seams and turn the end piece to the outside. Slipstitch the opening, as shown below.

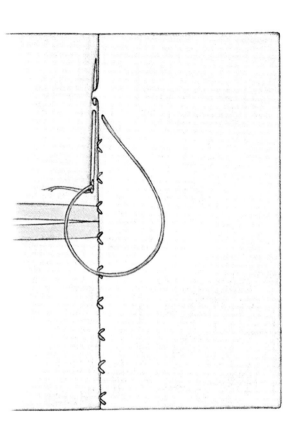

7 With the slipstitched side up and matching raw edges, center each accent/end piece on the short ends of one scarf body. Stitch, trim the seams, and press the seams toward the scarf body.

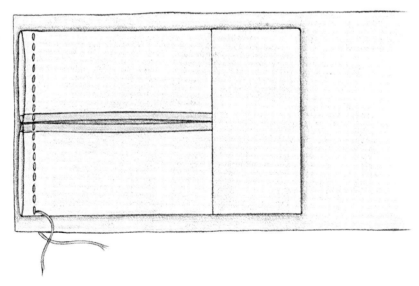

8 Fold the corners of each end piece to the center of the scarf and pin, as shown in the drawing at right. Folding the corners prevents catching in the seam when assembling the scarf. With right sides together, position the bottom scarf body over the top scarf. Sew around all sides, leaving about a 5-in. opening. Before trimming and clipping corners, bring the scarf to the outside and check that nothing has been caught and that the ends unfold freely. Then trim and clip. Turn the scarf to the outside. Slipstitch the opening.

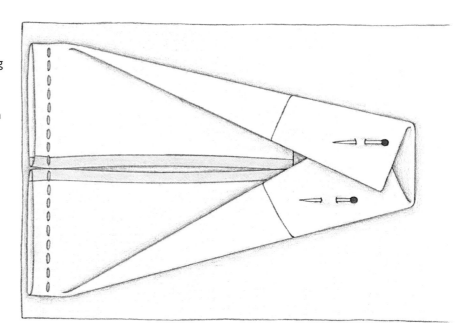

9 Sew a button or bead at the end of each accent trim strip.

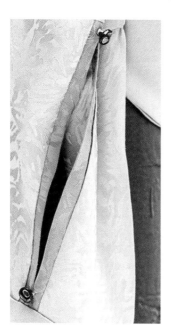

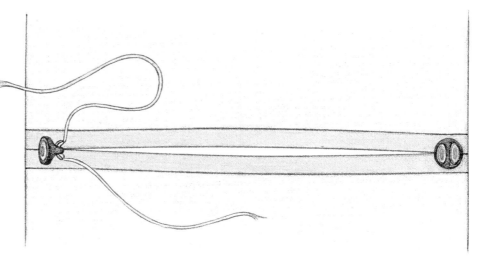

To wear, thread one end through the opposite opening. Cascade the ends attractively.

endless
reversible loop

*Literally two scarves in one, this is an endless loop
of pieced fabrics that reverses from one color scheme to
another. As easily as you can reach into the interior of the
scarf and turn it inside out (partially or completely), you'll
have a new look. Perfect for travelers, this accessory changes
dramatically from casual to formal or from neutral to
bright with a mere tug on the tube.*

finished size
60 in. by 5 in.

artist
Susan B. Allen

materials

- ⅔ yd. silk (primary fabric)
- ⅓ yd. each of five different silks (contrasting fabric)
- ¼ yd. light and dark stripe fabric
- Thread
- Rotary cutter and mat
- Basic sewing kit (see pp. 4-8)

fabric notes

See the sidebar on p. 137 for recommended fabrics.

cutting instructions

PRIMARY FABRIC
Cut 12 pieces 6 in. by 11 in.

FIVE ADDITIONAL FABRICS
Cut 12 assorted pieces 6 in. by 11 in.

ACCENT STRIPE
Cut four 11-in. strips against the direction of the stripe. The width of the strip should be determined by the width of the stripe. You want this to look like a series of squares after being pieced into the scarf. For example, if a black stripe is ½ in. wide, the distance between seams on the finished piece should also be ½ in. Therefore, cut each strip the width of one stripe plus 1 in. (two seam allowances) by 11 in.

1 Arrange the pieces in a pleasing order of colors on a flat surface using the primary fabric every other piece and alternating other mixtures. Insert a striped section about every six squares. Make a sketch of the pattern for reference. The drawing below shows Susan's layout for the scarf.

a	print #1
b	basic tone-on-tone stripe (light)
c	basic jacquard (black)
d	solid color
e	metallic
f	textured silk
g	print #2

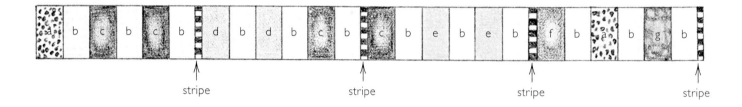

stripe   stripe   stripe   stripe

2 With right sides together and following the layout, sew one long edge of two adjacent pieces (see the drawing at right). Trim the seam and press open. Continue piecing fabric strips until all strips together equal 120 in. The distance between seams should be perfectly consistent from piece to piece or the scarf will hang with a tilt. To prevent this problem, choose one of the following methods:

a Measure and mark the corner seam-allowance points (below left).

or

b Lay each strip on a gridded surface (cutting mat or pressing board). Each piece must square up exactly with the previous piece (below right).

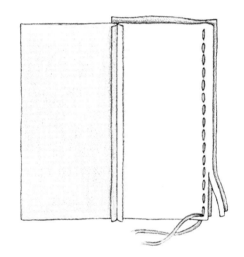

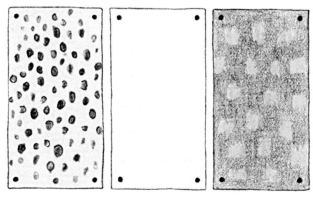

a

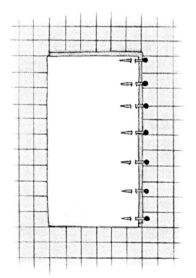

b

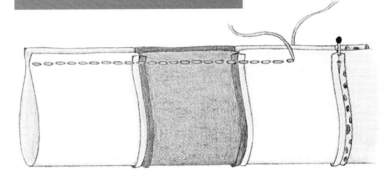

3 With right sides together, fold the pieced scarf in half lengthwise. Match the center of each cross seam and pin. Measure the same distance from the folded edge (it should be about 5 in.) and mark. Following these marks, draw a line the lengthwise distance of the scarf. Trim the seam allowance to an even $\frac{1}{2}$ in. Sew on this line (see the drawing above). Using a walking foot or hand-basting first will ensure good seam matching. Trim the seam and gently press the seam open for a soft press.

4 Turn the scarf inside out halfway only. Tucking the seam allowances to the inside, pin the two scarf ends together and slipstitch together, as shown in the drawing at right.

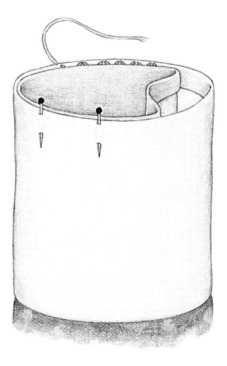

artist

Rochelle Harper

materials

SHORT VERSION

- ½ yd. 60-in.-wide mid-weight synthetic fleece
- ¼ yd. printed synthetic fleece

LONG VERSION

- 1 yd. 60-in.-wide mid-weight synthetic fleece
- ¼ yd. printed synthetic fleece

BOTH VERSIONS

- 32 washable glass beads with ³⁄₃₂-in. to ⅛-in. opening (optional)
- Thread
- Cardboard
- Basic sewing kit (see pp. 4-8)

fabric notes

Polartec is the recommended brand of synthetic fleece in both a solid and an allover print. The print is cut into strips to create a border on the scarf. The beads are used to embellish the optional tassels.

cutting instructions

SCARF BODY

See step 1 on p. 140 for details on preparing the scarf body.

BORDER

Measure the outer edges of the scarf and cut strips 2 in. wide or less on the crossgrain to equal this length. Your fabric motif will determine the appropriate width of the strips, but the trim should generally be kept under 2 in. for ease of use.

TASSELS

Cut four ¼-in.- to ⅜-in.-wide strips of either fleece on the crossgrain.

FACED OPENING

Cut one 4-in. by 1½-in. rectangle of the printed fleece.

hooded fleece

This warm and cuddly scarf features decorative borders outlining the inside of the hood and both ties. Easy-to-make self tassels finish the ends.

1 Both the short and long versions are cut on the crossgrain to take advantage of the easy stretch of the knit as it wraps around the body. The short version is cut using the length-wise fold as the top of the hood and the width of the fabric for the total length. The long version has a seam at the top of the hood. It is cut with the top of the hood along one selvage and uses two widths. The lengths of both versions are adjustable.

After determining the desired length of the scarf, use the drawing shown below as a guide for creating a pattern. The hood may be designed with a curved back seam extending from the center fold or seam or with a 90° angle.

I square = 2 in.

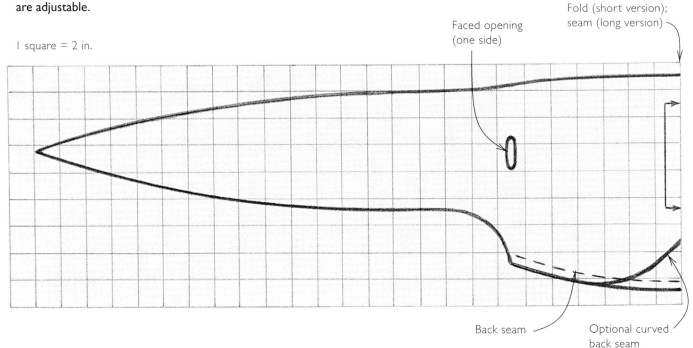

Faced opening (one side)

Fold (short version); seam (long version)

Back seam

Optional curved back seam

2 With right sides together, sew the top seam (if not cut on the fold). This seam may be stitched on a sewing machine or overlocked on a serger. Trim the seam to ⅜ in. When sewing, press the seam allowance open and topstitch on both sides of the seam. When serging, press the seam allowance to one side and topstitch one row of stitching.

3 Place the cord ends of the two small tassels on the right side of the fabric at the corner of the center back (see the sidebar on p. 143 for instructions on making tassels). Knot the cord inside the seamline to prevent the tassel from pulling out. With right sides together, stitch the back seam. Trim the seam allowance and repeat the topstitching as described in step 2.

4 Border strips may need to be pieced. Measure the upper and lower unfinished edges and piece the trim accordingly. With right sides together, stitch the short ends of the strips together. Trim the seam allowances. Be sure to match the design of the print when piecing the strips.

6 Turn the border to the inside of the scarf, favoring the outer scarf about ¼ in. Topstitch in the well of the seam through all layers. Draw a line on one border piece from the point through the center of the scarf tail and trim the excess fleece.

When sewing fleece, set the presser foot entirely on the fabric and offset the needle to the right to help control the fabric. Slightly stretch both layers as you sew to eliminate fabric tucks.

5 Beginning and ending at the points and with right sides together, loosely pin the border to the front long raw edge of the scarf. The ends of the border should extend slightly beyond the points of the scarf to sew a miter later. Sew the border in place using a long stitch and a narrow seam allowance. Trim the seam allowance close to the stitching line. Repeat to sew the bottom border.

7 To miter the points, fold the other border piece to meet the center line. Mark a ¼-in. seam allowance beyond the line and trim the excess fleece (a). Topstitch through the miter line (b).

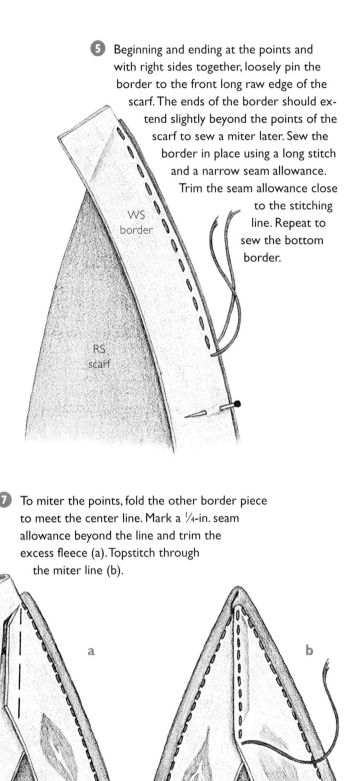

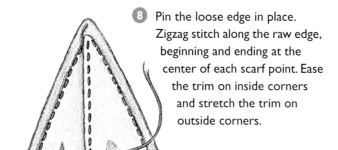

8 Pin the loose edge in place. Zigzag stitch along the raw edge, beginning and ending at the center of each scarf point. Ease the trim on inside corners and stretch the trim on outside corners.

9 Stitching from the border side of the scarf, free-motion stitch around the motifs of the print. This adds firmness to the edge and increases the textural quality. You may need to refer to the instruction manual of your sewing machine. (The technique is listed under embroidery or darning.)

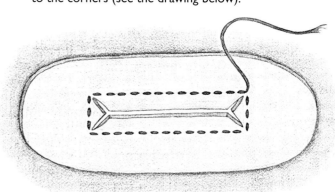

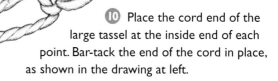

10 Place the cord end of the large tassel at the inside end of each point. Bar-tack the end of the cord in place, as shown in the drawing at left.

11 Following the pattern diagram and with right sides together, pin the faced-opening piece to the scarf. Stitch a narrow rectangle through both layers. Slash through the rectangle and clip to the corners (see the drawing below).

12 Trim the seam allowances close to the stitching line and turn to the inside. Finger-press the stitched edges flat and zigzag around the cut edge of the piece.

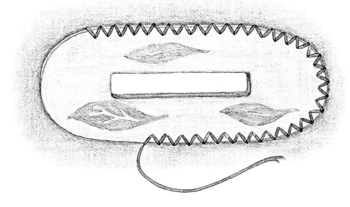

how to make the tassels

1 Stretch the fleece tassel strips until they lose most (if not all) of their stretch. If the strips break, cut the strips wider. If they are curling at the edges but not completely rolled, cut the strips narrower.

2 Using a piece of card-board about 4¾ in. square for the large tassels and a 2¾-in. square of card-board for the small tassels, wrap the fleece loosely around the card-board eight times. The cardboard squares are cut slightly larger than the desired finished tassel.

3 Braid or twist three 6-in. strands of fleece to make a cord. Pass the cord between the wrapped layers of fleece strips and tie securely at the top.

4 Cut the bottom ends of the tassel and remove from the cardboard.

5 Holding the tassel ends together, wrap a fleece strip tightly around the upper area of the tassel. Overlap the beginning of the strip and wrap to with-in ½ in. of the top. Thread the end of the strip in-to a large-eyed darn-ing or yarn needle and feed it through the center of the tassel, as shown at right. Cut off any extra length.

6 To add weight to the tassel, thread washable glass beads on half of the tassel strands. Then knot each strand below the bead. Each end of the tassel strands can be twisted to create a pointed end.

finished size
60 in. by 18 in.

artist
Bird Ross

materials
- 1¾ yd. each of two different silk or rayon fabrics (fabrics #1 and #2)
- ¾ yd. silk or rayon fabric (fabric #3)
- Two 1-in.-diameter buttons
- ½ yd., ½-in.-wide elastic
- Thread
- Basic sewing kit (see pp. 4-8)

fabric notes

Drapey rayons and silk in solids, prints, and stripes can be mixed together for an interesting effect. Use contrasting colors in brights and bolds or subtle monochromatics.

cutting instructions

SCARF BODY
Fabric #1: Cut one piece 61 in. by 19 in. (This measurement is determined by measuring over the shoulders from wrist to wrist. Adjust as necessary.)
Fabric #2: Cut one piece 61 in. by 19 in.

ENDS
Fabric #3: Cut four pieces 19 in. by 12 in.

TRIM
Fabric #3: Cut three pieces 42 in. by 2 in.
Fabric #1 or #2: Cut one 2-in. square. Cut the square in half diagonally to make two triangles.

POCKET
Fabric #1 or #2: Cut two pieces approximately 6 in. by 6 in.

scarf with sleeves

This scarf is an interesting tubular shape in three trimmed and buttoned fabrics. Secret openings with hidden pockets and gathered ends create optional sleeves and reinvent the use of a scarf.

1. Fold each trim strip in half lengthwise with the wrong sides together. Press.

2. On the right side of one scarf body and matching raw edges, pin the strips to the long edges. Starting at one end, pin one strip along one edge. Fold the exposed end diagonally and match the raw edges. Along the opposite long edge and starting at one end, pin one strip. Beginning at the other end, pin the second strip to the same long edge, overlapping the two strips for several inches. Allow one strip to project more than the other. Finish the raw ends as described above. Baste all strips in place.
   (See steps 1 and 2 of the Buttons and Buttonholes scarf on p. 123 for illustrations of this flat-piping technique.)

3. With right sides together, sew the two scarf bodies together at the long edges only. Sew with the basting stitches up to serve as a guide.

4. With wrong sides together, press the tubular scarf body so that the flat piped seams are in the center of the scarf, as shown below. Finish the raw edges of both ends of the tube.

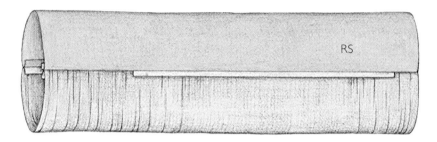

5. Press one long edge of each end piece ½ in. to the wrong side.

6. Pin the right side of one raw-edged triangle to the wrong side of the top center of each pressed end piece. Align the longest edge of the triangle ¼ in. from the folded edge.

7. Stitching through both layers, sew an almond-shaped circle large enough for a button to slip through. Clip through the center of the oval and to the ends of the almond shape. Pull the triangle through the opening to the right side of the scarf end. Press.

8. Starting with a line of stitching parallel to the opening, sew a concentric spiral around the opening until all of the triangle is sewn down. (See steps 10 through 12 of the Buttons and Buttonholes scarf on pp. 124-125 for illustrations of this buttonhole technique.)

9. Cut out two patch pockets in any shape, just large enough for your hand, keys and/or credit cards, and lipstick.

10. Finish the top edge of the pockets and press ½ in. to the wrong side. Make two stitched and faced buttonholes at the top and center of each pocket. Refer to the instructions above for this technique.

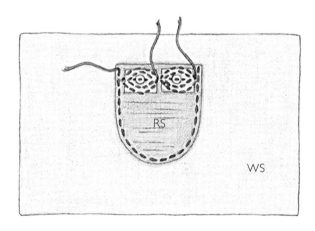

11. With wrong sides together, pin the pocket top 2 in. from one long edge of each unpressed end (these ends do not have a buttonhole). Using contrasting thread, sew around three sides of the pocket, leaving an opening at the top. Sew two buttons to each end piece to correspond with the buttonhole openings (see the drawing above).

12 With wrong sides together, pin one buttonhole end piece to each end piece that has a pocket, making sure that the buttonhole is centered over the pocket opening. Using French seams (see p. 13), sew both short sides. Press the seam allowance to one side.

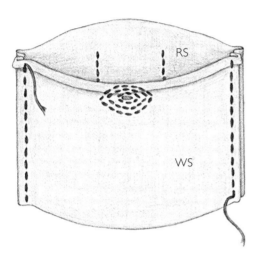

13 With right sides together and matching raw edges, pin one tubular end piece to each end of the scarf body. Center the buttonhole and the pocket over the flat-piped seam allowances of the scarf body. Stitch the pieces together, leaving a 5-in. opening at the button-hole area. Backstitch. Finish the seam allowances together and press toward the end piece. Edgestitch with contrasting thread except through the opening.

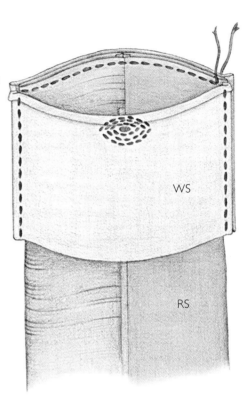

14 Finish the raw edge of each end. Press 1 in. to the wrong side. To make a casing, stitch ¾ in. from the folded edge, leaving a small opening to insert the elastic. Cut two pieces of elastic the circumference of your wrist plus ½ in. Feed one piece of elastic through each casing. Overlap ½ in. and zigzag to secure. Complete the casing stitching.

15 Sew a button to correspond with the buttonhole on each end piece, as shown in the drawing at right.

This scarf can be worn as a regular scarf loosely draped around your neck or with your hands through the holes and elastic ends. The ends can be left to hang free without elastic.

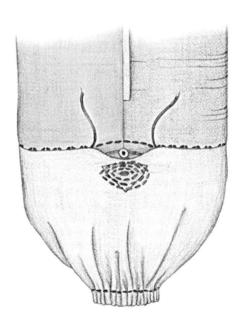

about the artists

susan b. allen

Susan B. Allen's theme is sensible innovation, whether she's working as a clothing designer, national speaker, or contributing editor to *Threads* magazine. A fabric lover, her line of clothing and accessories, which carries the label "Susan Allen Art," sells in shops across the United States. Through her consulting firm in Durham, North Carolina, Susan has presented over a thousand programs on creativity to corporate groups, and her work has been profiled on National Public Radio.

- **pieced squares (pp. 126-130)**
- **self-connecting squares (pp. 131-134)**
- **endless reversible loop (pp. 135-137)**

holly badgley

Holly believes that clothing is a very dramatic way of expressing oneself. She is influenced by ethnic fabrics and colors. She silk-screens, paints, and blends with thickened dyes, creating small semi-annual collections that concentrate on timeless, simple shapes that enhance her strong graphic story.

- **silk-screened velvet (pp. 111-115)**
- **painted silk (pp. 116-119)**

jean williams cacicedo

Jean Williams Cacicedo is a nationally renowned fabric artist and innovator. Her extraordinary Art Coats have been exhibited internationally in galleries, museums, and private collections. A frequent instructor at Penland and Split Rock summer fiber programs, she teaches regularly in Berkeley/San Francisco with The Sewing Workshop. Jean has been publishing in *Art to Wear, Art in America, Kimono Inspiration, Newsweek, American Craft,* and other magazines. She was a recipient of the National Endowment for the Arts crafts fellowship and actively shares her enthusiasm, skill, and abundant creativity in artwear. She maintains her studio and home in Berkeley, California.

- **slashed and felted (pp. 68-70)**
- **fringed wool crepe (pp. 71-73)**

jane conlon

Jane Conlon sews, writes, and teaches in Eugene, Oregon. The scarves created for this book were inspired by the richness and beauty of the materials used and express perpetual enchantment with the practical and creative challenges that sewing provides.

- **sari wrap (pp. 47-51)**
- **bead-embellished hem (pp. 76-78)**
- **beaded fringe (pp. 88-91)**

kathy davis

Kathy Davis has had an interest in sewing, tailoring, and fabric spanning the last 25 years. She assisted with design development and technical instructions for The Sewing Workshop Pattern Collection and with sample making for the *Vogue and Butterick's Designer Sewing Techniques* book and "Sewing Today" television series. Trained by The House of Lesage in Paris, Kathy has recently turned her attention to fine hand sewing and embroidery, as well as the book arts.

- **kimono patchwork (pp. 44-46)**
- **obi appliqué (pp. 54-57)**

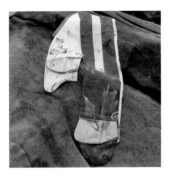

diane ericson

Diane's artistic explorations are fueled and challenged by a need to expand the creative process for herself and others. She loves the energy of bringing different techniques and materials together to learn about life through problem solving and transforming everyday objects...to see something new...to experience the magic!

- **knotted beads (pp. 79-83)**
- **stenciled and shaped (pp. 97-102)**

rochelle harper

Rochelle is a sewing instructor and author specializing in sportswear and outerwear. She spends her spare time renovating a circa 1912 bungalow and caring for her two girls in Portland, Oregon. She is author of *Sew the New Fleece* (The Taunton Press, 1997).

- **hooded fleece (pp. 138-143)**

karen morris

Karen Morris, a freelance editor and designer in Brookfield, Connecticut, is also a contributing editor at *Threads* magazine. She is inspired by the texture of fabric, the combination of subtle colors that are near one another on the color spectrum, or shades of the same color: water, the colors of water, the colors of light, transparency.

- **re-embroidered lace (pp. 30-32)**
- **punched Ultrasuede (pp. 60-61)**
- **dévoré velvet (pp. 88-91)**

joann pugh-gannon

Delicate, fine sewing has always been a passion of JoAnn Pugh-Gannon's, though it's not typical of her usual sewing projects or style of dress! To be able to create scarves using such techniques as cutwork, Madeira appliqué, and French machine sewing was a perfect way to express herself on the sewing machine and to add beautiful accessory pieces to her wardrobe.

- **heirloom sampler (pp. 38-40)**
- **cutwork linen (pp. 41-43)**
- **shadow-work silk (pp. 52-53)**

bird ross

Bird Ross has made up her own rules for sewing since she was a student in Mrs. White's Home Economics class nearly 30 years ago. Surrounded by intriguing materials and the desire to solve problems, Bird's sewing adventures continue in her studio in Madison, Wisconsin. She teaches and exhibits her sewing inspirations internationally.

- **woven "rags" (pp. 33-35)**
- **buttons and buttonholes (pp. 122-125)**
- **scarf with sleeves (pp. 144-147)**

carol spier

Carol Spier is a nonfiction editor who often produces books about the creative home arts. She enjoyed a first career as a theatrical costumer and laments that despite being in Manhattan five days a week, she rarely has time to get to its wonderful fabric shops.

- **simple quilted silk (pp. 94-96)**

marcy tilton

Marcy Tilton is an educator, writer, and artist, making her home and studio in southwestern Oregon. The founder of The Sewing Workshop, she teaches nationally. She writes for The Taunton Press and is a regular contributor to *Threads* magazine. Her expanding repertoire includes facilitating creativity workshops, exploring surface design, creating a line of jewelry and journals, and collaborating with fiber artists in design and pattern development.

- **remnant queen's ribbons (pp. 103-106)**
- **home away from home (pp. 107-110)**

stephanie valley

Stephanie's passion for creating and designing led her to a degree in surface design from the University of Kansas. She produces one-of-a-kind silk-screened and hand-stamped fabric yardage and a variety of artistic clothing and accessories. She is the set designer and prop director of the PBS television show "Sewing Today" and is the production director of The Sewing Workshop Pattern Collection. Stephanie is the author of *Sensational Sachets*.

- **floating flower (pp. 22-23)**
- **ribbon ladder (pp. 24-26)**
- **rolled rose border (pp. 27-29)**
- **laminated leaves (pp. 66-67)**
- **beaded pockets (pp. 84-87)**

resources

Ah! Kimono
4913 181st Place SW
Lynnwood, WA 98037
(206) 672-0842
Kimono and coordinated kimono sample packs

Apparel City
1330 Howard St.
San Francisco, CA 94103
(415) 621-6660
Tagboard

Britex
146 Geary St.
San Francisco, CA 94108
(415) 392-2910
Velvets, silks, rayon, wool jerseys and crepes, lace (mail order)

Dawn's Hide & Bead Away
203 N. Linn St.
Iowa City, IA 52245
(319) 338-1566
Beads and supplies; send $1.00 for catalog.

Dharma Trading Co.
1604 Fourth St.
San Rafael, CA 94915
(415) 456-1211
(800) 542-5227
Dyes, tools, craft essentials, fabrics for dyeing - mail order catalog

Exotic Silks
1959 Leghorn
Mountain View, CA 94043
(415) 965-7760
Silk fabrics in all weights

G Street Fabrics
12240 Wilkins Ave.
Rockville, MD 20852
(800) 333-9191
Velvets, silks, rayons, wool jersey, wool crepe, Ultrasuede, Portfolio sample program (mail order)

Jennifer Osner
58 Partridge Lane
Daly City, CA 94014
(415) 239-5896
Vintage including antique ribbons, lace, buttons, and tassels

Kasuri Dyeworks
1959 Shattuck Ave.
Berkeley, CA 94704
(510) 841-4509
Traditional Japanese fabrics

Mendel's Far-Out Fabrics
1556 Haight St.
San Francisco, CA 94117
(415) 621-1287
Double-faced cotton flannel underlining, velvet, exotic fabrics

Ruban et Fleur
Westchester Antiques Mall
8655 Sepulveda Blvd.
Westchester, CA 90045
(310) 641-3466
Modern and vintage silk, ombre, grosgrain, sheer and satin ribbon.

Rupert, Gibbon and Spider
P.O. Box 425
Healdsburg, CA 95448
(707) 433-9577
Fabric paint and dye, stamp carving tools

Seattle Fabrics
8702 Aurora Ave. North
Seattle, WA 98103
(206) 525-0670
Polartec fabric

Shipwreck Beads
2727 Westmoor Ct. S.W.
Olympia, WA 98502
(360) 754-2323
Beads and supplies; send $4.00 for catalog.

Silkpaint Corp.
P.O. Box 18
Waldron, MO 64092
(816) 891-7774
Fiber-Etch

Sweet Child of Mine
139 E. Fremont Ave.
Sunnyvale, CA 94087
(408) 720-8426
Petals hand dyed silk ribbon

Tandy Leather
Dept. T296PR
P.O. Box 791
Fort Worth, TX 76101
(817) 551-9771
Rotary leather punch tool; send $2.00 for mail-order catalog.

The Rain Shed
707 N.W. 11th St.
Corvallis, OR 97330
(541) 753-8900
Polartec fabric

Things Japanese
9805 N. E. 116th St., Suite 7160
Kirkland, WA 98034
(206) 821-2287
Fabric paints and dyes, silk thread, Dyeing in a Teacup kits

Welsh Products
932 Grant St.
P.O. Box 845
Benicia, CA 94510
(800) 745-3255
Thermal fax machines

Look for these and other *Threads* books
at your local bookstore or sewing retailer:

- Beyond the Pattern: Great Sewing Techniques for Clothing
- Couture Sewing Techniques
- Distinctive Details: Great Embellishment Techniques for Clothing
- 50 Heirloom Buttons to Make
- Fine Embellishment Techniques
- Fine Machine Sewing: Easy Ways to Get the Look of Hand Finishing and Embellishing
- Fit and Fabric
- Fitting Solutions: Pattern-Altering Tips for Garments that Fit
- Fitting Your Figure
- Great Quilting Techniques
- Great Sewn Clothes
- Jackets, Coats and Suits
- Just Pockets: Sewing Techniques and Design Ideas
- Quilts and Quilting
- The Sewing Machine Guide
- Sewing Tips & Trade Secrets
- Sew the New Fleece
- Shirtmaking
- Stitchery and Needle Lace
- Techniques for Casual Clothes

Books in the *Sewing Companion Library:*
- Easy Guide to Serging Fine Fabrics
- Easy Guide to Sewing Blouses
- Easy Guide to Sewing Jackets
- Easy Guide to Sewing Linings
- Easy Guide to Sewing Pants
- Easy Guide to Sewing Skirts

For a catalog of the complete line of *Threads* books and videos, write to:

The Taunton Press
P.O. Box 5506
Newtown, CT 06470-5506.

publisher
jim childs

acquisitions editor
jolynn gower

publishing coordinator
sarah coe

editor
peter chapman

designer
carol singer

photographer
jack deutsch

illustrator
christine erikson

typefaces
gill sans, new baskerville

paper
70-lb. patina

printer
**r. r. donnelley,
roanoke, virginia**